REPORTING, WRITING AND EDITING

JMC-03

Notes For

Post Graduate Diploma in Journalism and Mass Communication (PGJMC)

Useful For

IGNOU, KSOU (Karnataka), Bihar University (Muzaffarpur), Nalanda University, Jamia Millia Islamia, Vardhman Mahaveer Open University (Kota), Uttarakhand Open University, Kurukshetra University, Seva Sadan's College of Education (Maharashtra), Lalit Narayan Mithila University, Andhra University, Pt. Sunderlal Sharma (Open) University (Bilaspur), Annamalai University, Bangalore University, Bharathiar University, Bharathidasan University, HP University, Centre for distance and open learning, Kakatiya University (Andhra Pradesh), KOU (Rajasthan), MPBOU (MP), MDU (Haryana), Punjab University, Tamilnadu Open University, Sri Padmavati Mahila Visvavidyalayam (Andhra Pradesh), Sri Venkateswara University (Andhra Pradesh), UCSDE (Kerala), University of Jammu, YCMOU, Rajasthan University, UPRTOU, Kalyani University, Banaras Hindu University (BHU) and all other Indian Universities.

GullyBaba Publishing House Pvt. Ltd.

ISO 9001 & ISO 14001 CERTIFIED CO.

Regd. Office:
2525/193, 1st Floor, Onkar Nagar-A,
Tri Nagar, Delhi-110035
(From Kanhaiya Nagar Metro Station Towards Old Bus Stand)
Call: 9991112299, 9312235086
WhatsApp: 9350849407

Branch Office:
1A/2A, 20, Hari Sadan,
Ansari Road, Daryaganj,
New Delhi-110002
Ph.011-45794768
Call & WhatsApp:
8130521616,8130511234

E-mail: hello@gullybaba.com, **Website**: GullyBaba.com

New Edition

Author: Gullybaba.com Panel

About Publisher

Gullybaba Publishing House is the brainchild of Mr Dinesh Verma, his name alone evokes profound respect and admiration. He is the pioneer of providing quality materials to the students of IGNOU because, having been a student of IGNOU, he understood the difficulty and pain of the non-availability of quality materials himself. He is serving the students with the following services:

EXAM-SUCCESS GUIDES

Important questions, solved question papers, guess papers - all in one! to score good marks in lesser time and effort.

FREE BOOK

As our love and care for our students, here is a Free Gift – A Famous Book "Secrets to Pass IGNOU Exams with Less Study" for you. You can download it now! https://www.gullybaba.com/ignou-free/

YOUR CONTRIBUTION TO MOTHER-EARTH

When you read our books, you save our mother earth as we use recycled paper to make these books. On every purchase, we contribute something to plant a plant.

SOLVED ASSIGNMENTS PDFs / HAND-WRITTEN

Best and genuine solved assignments PDFs you can instantly download from Gullybaba.com or our App.

PROJECT REPORTS/SYNOPSIS

Best Quality No-Rejection projects/synopsis by professionals researchers in ready to refer format.

MOBILE APP

You can download 'Gullybaba' app from Google Play Store to enjoy all above services at one place.

Why Gullybaba's IGNOU Help Books

Is Fear of Exams making you stressful? Are you not getting good marks in your IGNOU exams? Are you looking for sure-shot solution get ahead in your IGNOU studies? Look no further than the answer: Gullybaba.com! With our expertly crafted course help-books, you'll be ready to face any exam with ease-guaranteed. What's more, we offer a huge discount on IGNOU Help Books Combo Deals – Save BIG.

Now, complete IGNOU courses more quickly and with Good Marks in Lesser Time & Effort.

Home Delivery of GPH Books

You can order Gullybaba Books online from Gullybaba.com or Gullybaba App. We dispatch books on the same day of receiving the order through our fastest courier partners.
You can also order books through WhatsApp on 9350849407 or by email at order@gullybaba.com.
We also provide "Cash On Delivery" through our courier partners and sometimes Govt. Postal Department.

Important Note to Sellers

Selling this book on any online platform like Amazon, Flipkart, Shopclues, Rediff, etc. without prior written permission of the publisher is prohibited and hence any sales by the SELLER will be termed as ILLEGAL SALE of GPH Books which will attract strict legal action against the offender.

Notable Information

An attempt has been carefully made to present this book more useful and meet the requirement and challenges of the course prescribed by IGNOU University. We hope that this effort will fulfil the readers' expectations and help them excel in exams. Referring to University study material alongside this book is like "icing on the cake".

We wish you a successful and rewarding career. If you have any feedback to improve our books/products, please email at feedback@gullybaba.com. Because we believe, "Feedback is breakfast of champions" and our readers are our strength.

Table of Contents

Question Papers

NEWS REPORTING

INTRODUCTION

In every newsroom, journalists constantly apply what's called news judgement: the ability to determine which stories are most interesting and important to readers. News stories most often appear in the front section of a newspaper. The main purpose of a news story is to report the news in an objective manner. This means that the author of the news story should not include his or her own opinions in the article. The author should tell the readers what has occurred, but should stick to the facts. News reporting is professional work. One needs to acquire skills, polish the language of work and ground oneself well into the various social, economical and political issues of the society. Most news stories revolve around some sort of conflict – conflicts involve opposing opinions. All of the sides involved in the conflict must be given a chance to have their say. If this does not happen, the news report is neither balanced nor fair. In reality, however, it is almost impossible for a news story to be completely objective, no matter how hard the reporter tries to make it so. There are many factors in news story that can imply bias, either intentionally or not.

Q1. Define "the news". What are the types of news?

Ans. News is a report of a current event. It is information about something that has just happened or will happen soon. News is a report about recent happenings in a newspaper, television, radio or internet. News is something that is not known earlier. In common parlance, news is what is new. A news is what everyone wants to know about. A newspaper office's main concern is to gather and report news—local, state, regional, national and international. The basic understanding about news is essential for any editorial work in a newspaper/news agency/ news magazine.

It is said that the letters in the word "NEWS" is derived from the four directions as indicated below:

- N–North
- E–East
- W–West
- S–South

This shows that news can come from anywhere. News is the report of a current event, something that was not known, information of recent events and happenings. According to John B. Bogart, City editor of the New York '*Sun*', the news is, "when a dog bites a man, that is not news; but when a man bites a dog, that is news". He pointed out very correctly that unusual events fall under the purview of the news.

Another famous editor of the *Sun,* defined the news as, "...everything that occurs, everything which is of sufficient importance to arrest and absorb the attention of the public or of any considerable part of it".

The definition of a news item is dependent on:

- The size of the community (readers)
- The periodicity of the publication (Weekly, daily etc.)
- The social character and economic base of the Community
- The focus of attention or emphasis of the Community (e.g. a provincial city's municipality election may not become headline in the newspapers of Delhi or Calcutta).

According to Joseph Pulitzer the publisher of the New York World, he defined news as, "original, distinctive, dramatic, romantic, thrilling, unique, curious, quaint, humorous, odd and apt-to-be-talked-about".

According to Walter William, the news as, "...News, in its broadest sense, is that which is of interest to the readers—the public...".

The former managing editor of the New York Times said that the news was "...anything you can find out today that you didn't know before".

The news is mainly divided into two main categories – Hard and Soft news.

(1) Hard News: Hard news is the kind of fast-paced news that usually appears on the front page of newspapers. Stories that fall under the umbrella of hard news often deal with topics like business, politics and international news. It is mostly event-centered. It is a narration of an event. The Hard news items are centered on, "What, when, where and why". The following news item taken from the front page of The Times of India, Delhi, Thursday, December 5, 2013.

Two Toddlers Killed in Accidents

> Bangalore: Two toddlers were killed in separate accidents in the city. Around 8.30am on Wednesday, two-and-a-half year-old Dhanushri, who was sitting on the fuel tank of a motorcycle driven by her uncle, was killed after a mini-truck hit the bike near Hoodi Circle, off KR Puram. Her five-month pregnant mother was riding pillion.
>
> Suresh, the rider, and Nagalakshmi, the mother, survived the accident with injuries. Suresh said they were going to the Ayyappa temple in KR Puram, where Nagalakshmi's husband, also Suresh, was waiting for them. Nagalakshmi's husband runs a provision store in Whitefield and was to go on a pilgrimage to the temple town of Sabarimala on Wednesday night. The family was slated to take part in special prayers at the temple.

(2) Soft News: Soft news is often called human-interest news because it concentrates on individuals as people rather than as citizen. It is background information or human-interest stories as arts, entertainment and lifestyles were considered soft news. A soft news story tries instead to entertain or advise the reader. They would like to enter beneath the upper crust of hard news. This type of news is called soft news. The following news item taken from 'The Times of India, Wednesday, December 4, 2013.

YouTube Home Page Goes Down

The home page of world's most popular video sharing website YouTube went down for a while today. The web page showed that the site was facing the 500 internal server errors. This error means that the website is facing issues at server level, but a more specific reason for the problem has not been ascertained yet. Upon clicking YouTube, the visitor got this message: "500 Internal Server Error. Sorry, something went wrong. A team of highly trained monkeys has been dispatched to deal with this situation.

Q2. List various elements that make an event a 'news' and hence worthy of reporting for a newspaper/news agency.

Ans. News items have some particular features. Some of them are discussed below:

- **Timeliness:** News has short life and must be timely. It will not be news if it is already known or reported long after its happening. A train accident happens on Monday will not be news on Thursday.
- **Nearness or Proximity:** The community, the reader, is more interested in what happens in his locality, village, town or country rather than in distant places. A football match in New York will not be of any interest to the people in Mumbai. People are more interested in the news which has an immediate impact on them. Rise in milk prices in Orissa will be of no interest to the readers in Delhi.
- **Conflict:** Conflicts of all types make news. It may be clash between two rival gangs or groups of people in a street or conflict between two countries, they are news.
- **Prominence:** The prominence of the person involved in an event or in any occurrence enhances the value of news. Assassination of US President will make the world headlines, but the murder of a village chief may be carried only in a local daily.
- **Government Action:** A government order, action or announcement makes news. The Indian government decision on giving most favoured nation status to Pakistan makes news.

- **Development Projects and Issues:** Progress in any development projects or some developments in an issue make news. Completion of Dadri power plant in Uttar Pradesh makes news. Similarly, the India Government's invitation to Kashimiri separatists for talks makes news.
- **Human Interest:** A happening or an event if is of human interest, that will be news. The death of the tallest person in the world makes news.
- **Weather and Sports:** The weather and the sports make news. Newspapers take arrival of monsoon or cyclones news on front page. Newspapers have separate section for sports.
- **Follow-up:** Follow-up and update of some events or on issues make news. The development two days after a plan crash will make news-what the probe over the accident says, what the government action over it and how the families of victims have been affected- is news.

Q3. Describe "the news values" which a news reporter should keep in mind for determining whether an event is newsworthy or not.

Or

Mention qualities required for good news.

Ans. News values, sometimes called news criteria, determine how much prominence a news story is given by a media outlet, and the attention it is given by the audience. A. Boyd states that: "News journalism has a broadly agreed set of values, often referred to as 'newsworthiness'..." News values are not universal and can vary widely between different cultures. In a country where there is no freedom of the press, and a dictator or an authoritarian ruler is ruling the country, a news against the government will never be published. But in countries like India and the US, newspapers can report anything under the sun if they have the authentic source to support whether it goes against the Prime Minister or the President. However, while reporting news the reporters and newspapers should not be careful in their use of words and that should not be derogatory which is unethical as well. Also a news item, which may be news worthy for a community, will not be carried by a newspaper if it is of no interest to its readers.

Fundamental Qualities of the News: Reporters have a busy schedule. Many a time, they do not get sufficient time to write the story after collecting all the facts. So, they work in haste. They are left with very little time to write, type or key in their stories. But even in such a situation, reporters should keep in mind that the reader will enjoy a good story. A story written well in style will catch and retain the attention of the reader. Though it is generally said that news reports have a life span of only 24 hours, readers will remember such stories for a long time.

A good news report should have the following qualities:

- **Accuracy:** News should be accurate. When we fail in accuracy, we lose credibility. Reporter and people involved in writing and editing news should always cross check facts and information. People are greatly offended by misspelled names. Rumours or gossips should not be given in news.
- **Balance:** News report should always be balanced. If it is about a controversy, both sides of the story should be presented. When reporting a strike, for instance, give the claim of the authorities and also that of the workers on how far it is successful. If it is a 'hartal', go around the spot and observe the exact position. A story may appear to be imbalanced, and thus biased, if it has too much of government views, or tends to give too much of foreign news which has little relevance to the readers.
- **Objectivity:** Reporter should be objective in their writing. Facts and people's opinions should be presented without mutilations. News should not take sides.
- **Clarity:** A report is read by many people in society. It should be in simple language and written with clarity. It should not be ambiguous. It should satisfy the reader's inquisitiveness. Facts that are not clear to the readers should be avoided. It is said that when the reporter when is in doubt, he should leave it out.
- **Impact:** New items should have some impact. News about a dilapidated and overused bridge in time to move the authorities to take up repairs may help avert a tragedy. Reporter should develop a "nose for news", particularly news that will make a positive impact.

Q4. Define News Values. List the points used by a journalist to judge newsworthiness.

Or

Write a short note on News Values.

Ans. News values differ from community to community, country to country. While reporting such events, you should be careful not to appear to be derogatory in tone or in content. Similarly, news values are different for developing and developed countries. For the industrialized and individualized societies of developed countries, communally provocative speeches and incidents may be reported word for word, blow by blow.

Journalists are the best judges about what is news and what is not. They take this decision based on certain news values. The following are the salient points to judge the newsworthiness:

- **Timeliness:** News is something new. So timeliness is a great factor in deciding news. An incident that happened one month back will not make news for today's newspaper. Also timeliness varies from publication to publication. For a newspaper, events that had happened on the previous day is news. But for a weekly, events of the previous one week can make news. For a 24-hour television news channel, every second is a deadline. They can break the news anytime. So their timeliness is different from that of a newspaper.
- **Impact:** Impact of an event decides its newsworthiness. When the tsunami waves struck several parts of the world, thousands of people were affected. It became major news for the whole world. But if a cyclone kills 20 people in Bangladesh, it may not have any impact on other parts of the world. When dengue fever affects 100 people in Delhi, it makes news not only in Delhi but in other states also because the impact is more wide and people become more alert about the news.
- **Proximity:** "Bird flu spreading and hundreds of chicken dying in England". Does it make news for you? You may read it but do not worry about it. But bird flu spreading in West Bengal will make you alert. This is because it is in your proximity. A plane crash in Peru will not be big news in India, but if an aircraft crashes in India, it will be headlines everywhere. So proximity decides the news.
- **Controversy:** People like controversies. Anything that is connected with conflicts, arguments, charges and counter-charges, fights and tension becomes news. All of you might

have heard of Kargil. It was a conflict between India and Pakistan. It became great news all over the world. Many of you may remember the controversy about the Indian and Australian cricket teams. It was news for all the media. When terrorists crashed their plane into the World Trade Centre in New York it was lead news everywhere.

- **Prominence:** If a prominent person is involved in any event, it becomes news. If an ordinary person's car breaks down and he has to wait for ten minutes on the roadside till the vehicle is repaired it makes no news. But if the Prime Minister's car breaks down and his motorcade has to stop for five minutes it becomes news. A person visiting Rajghat and paying homage to Gandhiji may not be a news item, but when the US President visits Rajghat it becomes news.
- **Currency:** News is about current events. Suppose the Olympic Games are held in India. It becomes news because everybody is interested in it. Likewise when SAARC leaders meet in Delhi to formulate future action plans, it becomes the current news. Similarly, if extreme cold weather continues for a week and fog disrupts air, rail and road traffic, it becomes news.
- **Oddity:** Unusual things makes news. Extraordinary and unexpected events generate public interest. You might have seen box items in newspapers about such happenings. A man pulls a car by his hair, a woman gives birth to triplets, a singer enters the Guinness Book by singing non-stop for 48 hours, the painting of a famous artist is auctioned for a very expensive price. All such odd stories evoke much public interest.
- **Emotion:** Stories of human interest make good news items. *For e.g.* The police rescue a school boy kidnapped by mischief makers after a search of two weeks. The parents meet the boy in an emotionally surcharged atmosphere. The story of this meeting with a photograph makes a good human interest report. Doctors advise a girl in Pakistan to undergo a heart surgery urgently. But her parents cannot afford the expenses. The Rotary Club of Delhi east offers help through their scheme of 'Gift of Life'. The girl comes to India and undergoes surgery successfully. While going back she and her overwhelmed

parents narrate their experiences in India. This makes a good human interest story.

- **Usefulness:** Sometimes news items help the public in various ways. You must have noticed that weather forecasters warn fishermen not to go to the sea for fishing on certain days because of rough weather. Newspaper gives the phone numbers of police stations, hospitals, ambulance services etc. to help people. You might have seen in newspapers, requests from relatives to donors of blood for a patient in a critical condition. Newspapers also raise funds from the public to help victims of disasters and natural calamities, like tsunami and earthquake.
- **Educational value:** News has also an educational value. In almost all newspapers, you can find columns about educational and job opportunities. These guide you about different educational courses, career options available, opportunities for higher studies etc. These news items help you become more knowledgeable.

Q5. Identify the main sources of news.

Ans. News can be collected from different sources. A reporter, to be successful, should have a variety of reliable and highly placed contacts. They are some of the useful "sources" for his information. Among the news sources, some are available to all reporters, such as Public meetings, monitoring of radio and television programmes, press conferences, news briefings, seminars and other functions. Contacts with top officials in government, political parties or in business are sources of exclusive information for the reporter.

Sometimes a valuable tip-off may come from an ordinary person such as the driver of a minister's personal car. Some of the contacts may like to be quoted for the story as it gives them publicity. In case of a critical story, they may not risk their neck. In that case, the story may have to be distributed to 'sources' only. It is the responsibility of a reporter to ensure the truthfulness of a report. In such cases, it will be advisable to keep some documents (copies) or/and audio tape to prove the news when needed.

A reporter may face the confrontation with the government or political leaders or some group members while collecting news particularly of critical and investigate nature. A reporter should dare to face such situations. He should also treat his sources as "sacred". There may be pressure from the sources, reporter should protect sources at any cost.

An editorial in the Washington Post on December 17, 1971 by Executive Editor, Bejamin Bradley is still relevant today.

Over the last five years, the reporters and editors of this newspaper have become increasingly concerned about the use and abuse of the unattributable information by the government at background briefings. In theory, unattributed information given to the press by the governmental background briefings enables the press to do a better job of reporting. In practice, this is less and less true. Background briefings have become the vehicles for the government to give its versions of the news, to use the press as a vehicle for its policy announcements .and its political advantage without taking responsibility for what it is saying. This practice has been the of every administration. The Washington Post, newspaper has long been a party to this practice. The public has suffered from this collusion between the government and the press.

Therefore, it is now the policy of the Washington Post in its coverage of government news briefings, to insist on public accountability for the public business. We instructed our reporters to insist through every means available to them that material offered at these briefings should be on record and fully attributable. If ground rules are imposed providing for anything less than full attribution on the record, Washington Post reporters will immediately say that attribution be made direct on the record. If that request is refused, the reporter will seek attribution specific enough so that no reader can reasonably be confused. If this request is refused, the Washington Post has instructed its reporters to inform the agency or official that the newspaper's handling of the material will be determined by the editors' judgment of their responsibility to inform the public. We believe that responsibility cannot be transferred by us to any public official or circumscribed by government edict. The Washington Post believes that while certain circumstances may make full on-the-record attribution impractical, the public interest is not served by permitting statements of policy to be made by government officials who are unwilling to be held accountable for their own words. The decision whether to remain voluntarily in the briefing is one for the reporter's discretion, under normal conditions, he would remain and report under these guidelines. Nothing in this policy concerns contacts with government officials and other news sources, initiated by reporters of Washington Post. In these instances, the contacts will continue on an independent, individual basis, under terms understood and accepted by the reporter and the news source.

Q6. Define the Lead and the Body in news reporting.

Or

Write a short note on Lead.

Ans. A news story is written in various formats. Basically, the story is divided into lead, body and then conclusion. The **lead** is the beginning, the most important structural element of a story. Charnley (1966) stated that, "an effective lead is a brief, sharp statement of the story's essential facts". The lead is usually the first sentence or in some cases the first two sentences and is ideally 20-25 words in length. The top loading principles applies to the lead, but the unread ability of long sentences constraints its size. This makes writing a lead an optimization problem, in which the goal is to articulate the most encompassing and interesting statement that a writer can make in one sentence, given the material in which s/he has to work. A good lead should arouse the reader's curiosity and egg him on to read the rest of the story. It should be precise, crisp and made up of short, simple sentences.

Rudyard Kipling, who worked as a journalist with the then British-owned "Pioneer" during the Raj days, wrote:

I keep six honest serving men
(They taught me all I knew),
Their names are What and Why and When
And How and Where and Who.
I send them over land and sea,
I send them east and west;
But after they have worked for me
I give them all a rest.

The lead should answer the five W's-Who, What, Where, When and Why-and How. A few examples are given below:

- **The Who Lead:** In who lead, a person will be focus of the news. For example, Mr. Suraj Bandookwala, 65, an industrialist and former President of the Indian Gunmaker's Association, died in the J.J. Hospital in Bombay on Monday morning after a prolonged illness. He suffered from lung cancer and had undergone surgery both in India and USA.

- **The What Lead:** In what lead, the incident or the event will be the focus of the news. For example, the collision between two buses of the Delhi Transport Undertaking on the Ridge on Friday, killing five passengers and injuring 14 others, was attributed by an official spokesman to poor visibility due to heavy rains.
- **The Where Lead:** In where lead, the focus will be on the place. For example, the hill town of Shimla in Himachal Pradesh lay under a blanket of snow on Tuesday morning after heavy snowfall over-night.
- **The When Lead:** In when lead, the centre of the news is the time. For example, almost at the same moment that the Prime Minister was assuring agitated members of the Lok Sabha about a definite improvement in the situation in terrorist-hit Kashmir, the Home Minister at a press conference was expressing grave concern about the escalation in violence.
- **The Why Lead:** In why lead, the reason behind the incident is the focus. For example, a boy and a girl both in their teens, committed suicide by consuming poison in a Delhi hotel on Sunday because their parents objected to their plan to marry.
- **The How Lead:** In how lead, how the incident happened becomes the focus of the news. For example, a Japanese mountaineer was trapped in a blizzard 150 kilometres from Kathmandu and died on Thursday before rescue teams could reach the spot.

While the lead should arouse the reader's interest, the **body** should sustain it. The body should flow smoothly and logically from the lead. It should expand each of the pointes mentioned in the lead and, as far as possible, in the same order. The body should be as complete and as tight as possible. It should provide all the relevant information within the shortest space possible. Brevity and simplicity should be the basic principle. Do not use two words where one word can be used. A good reporter should always keep his ears and eyes open. He should know where to go for the news and facts he requires for the story. A good reporter should also recognise news when he encounters it and select the vital points for inclusion in his story. He should spend time visiting places and meeting people his potential sources of news.

Q7. What is Reporting? Enumerate the various types of reporting.

Or

Write a short note on Objective reporting.

Ans. The core of reporting is news gathering. A report is a news article or broadcast, which gives information about something that has just happened. Reportage is the reporting of news and other events of general interest for newspapers, television or radio. By far the best definition of reporting has been given by George A. Hough, the Professor of The University of Georgia, he says, Reporting is a journalist's word for research, for the collection of data, for the gathering of facts. This research is topical. It deals with current events, contemporary issues and people. Reporting is the art, the skill, the business, and the profession of gathering information for immediate use.

Based on the topics and nature of news, there are different types of reporting. These are as follows:

(1) Objective Reporting: Reporting of news, unlike editorial writing, is often described as a coldly impersonal job. A reporter is essentially a story teller and he should tell the story in an objective and truthful manner, without lacing it with personal opinions or subjective comments. He should be fair, impartial and present both sides of the story. Complete objectivity is not possible. It is a mere concept. The reporter is a human being, not a robot and he has certain ideas, feelings, attitudes, opinions and prejudices. However, a good reporter should try to rise above them and tell the facts as he has collected them in his search for truth.

No responsible reporter would behave like the American journalist, Janet Cooke, who won the prestigious Pulitzer Prize in 1980 for a story about drugs which was later proved to be fictional and fictitious. The journalist committed a deliberate fraud by dramatising a fake scene in which an eight year-old boy is injected with heroin supplied by the lover of the boy's mother.

A national newspaper carried on its front page that there was a "mass rape" at a students' function in a Madhya Pradesh town. After the report appeared on the front page of the newspaper it caused a sensation. The Editor asked a reporter of the news item, who insisted that the mass rape had happened. By corroboration he produced a number of eye-witnesses.

However, when they were cross-examined and asked specifically to reveal only what they had seen, they baffled and the investigator soon realised that the reporter had written the story on the basis of a gossip and filed it without verifying the facts. All that had happened was that during a function to celebrate the annual day of a local college, a portion of the shamiana came down, the electricity got cut off and a few students entered the women's enclosure and molested some of the girls.

The next day the cub reporter submitted a stop which ran as follows:

"Mrs. Gulab Paniwala, alleged wife of Mr. Rakesh Paniwala, who claims to be the mayor of Shangrila, gave a cocktail party at her house in Model Town on Monday to bid farewell to Mrs. Jyoti Jariwala, reported to be the wife of the well-known industrialist, Samar Jariwala. Among those present at the party were Mrs. Romi Puriwala, said to be the widow of the late Hansraj Puriwala, former cabinet minister, along with her alleged offspring, Jani Puriwala," and so it went on.

The reporter had quite clearly gone to the other extreme in writing this report which was quickly consigned to the waste paper basket.

Reporters must check and cross-check the facts from different sources until he is absolutely sure of them. Only then he should write the story. The golden rule of reporting tells the truth. Of course, objective reporting is not synonymous with dullness. It means fair and impartial reporting that is free from personal bias or prejudice.

(2) Interpretative Reporting: Interpretative reporting, combines facts with interpretation. It delves into reasons and meanings of a development. It is the interpretative reporter's task to give the information along with an interpretation of its significance. In doing so he uses his knowledge and experience to give the reader an idea of the background of an event and explain the consequences it could led to. Besides his own knowledge and research in the subject, he often has to rely on the opinions of specialists to do a good job.

According to D. MacDongall, the author of a book **Interpretation Reporting**, the first important inputs to interpretative reporting was provided by World War-I. When the First World War broke out, most Americans were taken by surprise. They were utterly unable to explain its causes. This led changes in the style of reporting. The result was that when in 1939 the Second World War began, an overwhelming majority of the Americans expected it or at least knew it was possible.

MacDongall says that a successful journalist should be more than a thoroughly trained journeyman. With his reading of history, economics, sociology, political science and other academic subjects, an interpretative reporter is aware of the fact that a news item is not an isolated incident, but an inevitable link to a chain of important events. An interpretative reporter cannot succeed if he hampered by prejudices and stereotyped attitudes, which would bias his perception of human affairs. Interpretative reporting thus goes behind the news, brings out the hidden significance of an event and separates truth from falsehood.

Example (i): The biennial elections to the Rajya Sabha took place in July. The interpretative reporter would give the reader the breakup of the results and acquaint him with the impact they would have on the various political parties and on the composition of the Upper House. He would, for instance, inform the reader that the Congress Party lost its majority in the Rajya Sabha, following the elections and that the Bharatiya Janata Party emerged as the main opposition, pushing the Janata Dal to third place. He will then explain the effect it would have on the working of the Rajya Sabha and on political party affairs generally.

Example (ii): The election of the new President of India took place in July. The interpretative reporter would not only convey the bare news of the victory of Dr. Shankar Dayal Sharma but, analyse the reasons behind it and reflect on the consequences of his victory for the future of the Congress and opposition parties.

(3) Investigative Reporting: It is difficult to define the term "investigative" journalism. Some newspapers scoff at the very idea of an investigative journalist. In one way, "investigative" journalism is a redundant concept, since all stories require some kind of investigation on the part of the reporter. However, the investigative reporter is expected to dig deeply beyond the facts stated in the hard news. Though we may face difficulty in defining the term, we cannot ignore the concept of investigative journalism. Many journalism students have an ambition to become "investigative" reporters. An "investigative" journalist sees himself as the conscience of society, pursuing corruption in high places without fear or favour. In his book Press and Law (Vikas, New Delhi 1990), Justice A.N. Grover has quoted from the forward of Investigative reporting by Clark R. Mollevhogg. According to the Foreword, investigative reporting has three elements:

(i) It has to be the own work of the reporter. Under no circumstance should it be of others;

(ii) The subject of the reporting should be such that it is of importance for the readers to know; and

(iii) There must not be any attempt made to hide the truth from the people.

In western countries, investigative reporting has made great leaps. Nevertheless, in India, it is still in its infancy. Most Indian newspapers do not allocate the manpower and funds necessary for a first-rate investigative job. According to one eminent Indian Editor, attempts at investigative reporting, to quote one eminent Indian editor, are like drilling for oil. A fair amount of wastage of effort has to be taken for granted. But when the oil is discovered and becomes marketable, the sense of achievement is usually more than in any other sector of journalistic enterprise.

In India, investigative reporting started making a mark after the end of the internal emergency in 1997, particularly through the reports published in The Indian Express.

In our country, investigative reporters have brought to light a number of scandals– the Bhagalpur blinding incidents by the police, Kuo oil deal, A. R. Antulay's private trusts, the securities scam involving Indian and foreign banks and stock brokers, etc. An enterprising reporter once got himself arrested so that he could give a first-hand account of life in Delhi's Tihar Jail.

With governments becoming increasingly secretive and corruption spreading its tentacles far and wide, the need for investigative reporting cannot be over emphasised. Yet we must remember that investigative reporting is not everybody's cup of tea. It requires hard and sustained work. The investigative reporter should be a combination of a crusader, super detective and blood hound and he should have the necessary time and finance to carry out his work. The best kind of investigative reporting is that which keeps the public interest in mind. It may highlight an injustice, expose corrupt practices or unmask dishonest politicians and bureaucrats.

(4) Crime Reporting: Crime is the most important beat in the profession of journalism. Crime reporting is not separate from the objective, interpretative and investigative form of reporting. Here it is separately dealt with because it is a separate and important beat in all big and medium level daily newspapers. There is a tremendous public interest in crime stories and no newspaper can afford to ignore them without damage to its circulation and credibility. Attempts made by some newspapers to keep crime out of their columns, proved to be counterproductive and were soon abandoned.

Crime is a part of life and it is a newspaper's duty to inform the readers of what crimes are going on in their city, state or country. However, crime reporting should not him at satisfying morbid curiosity or sensation mongering. Junior reporters generally cover crime, but it is a highly responsible and speacialised job. The reporter should have good contacts in the police and other departments of administration as well as a working knowledge of the penal codes and law on libel and other relevant matters.

The crime reporter has to follow a code conduct. He should be as objective as is humanly possible and avoid resorting to sensationalism or cheap gimmicks to catch the attention of the readers. He should not suppress news of public interest, nor should he seek to settle personal scores with police officers or lawyers of judges. He must be careful that in the course of this work, he does not unnecessarily invade a citizen's privacy.

People sometime criticise crime reporting by the press. Some reporters have also been found following unethical standards, thus causing much pain and sorrow to the victims or their families and friends.

(i) **Crime as News:** There are several types of crime news–murders, fires, accidents, robberies, burglaries, fraud, blackmail, kidnapping, rape, etc.

(ii) **Fires:** The reporter must get his facts correct about the essential elements of a fire story–the number of persons killed or injured, the extent of damage to property, the loss of valuables, etc. He must also find out if the fire brigade responded in time or was guilty of delaying the fire-fighting operations through sheer lethargy or incompetence or a lack of water supply. He should question eye-witness about any acts of bravery or cowardice. All these are essential ingredients of a fire story.

The lead in a fire story would normally suggest itself. If, for instance, lives have been lost, it needs highlighting in the lead. Where possible, list the names of the dead and the injured.

Example: A major fire caused extensive damage to New Delhi's Vigyan Bhavan, the premier venue of international and national conferences, on Monday night. A chowkidar on duty received minor burns. According to preliminary investigations, the fire broke out in 'the kitchen and soon spread to other rooms on the ground floor. The chowkidar raised an alarm which alerted the head clerk on duty who informed the fire brigade and the police. Ten fire tenders soon arrived on the scene. However, their fire-fighting operations were hampered by lack of water in the hydrants. By the time water tankers rushed to the site, the fire had engulfed a large area and damaged files, furniture, curtains and ceilings.

(iii) Homicides: In cases of a major murder, the reporter should rush to the scene as soon as possible after receiving a tip and gather all the relevant facts. In nine cases out of ten, crime reporters in, say, Delhi, depend on police information about murders and there is a time lapse before they can begin their investigations.

In reporting dowry deaths or alleged dowry deaths, for instance, the reporter should refrain from levelling uncorroborated statements by one party or the other. He must therefore get his facts correct– by talking to the investigating police officer, the girl's in-laws and her parents, and, if possible, the neighbours.

Example: A 25 year old housewife, Sushmita Malik, died in Pant Hospital on Monday morning from burns received in a kitchen fire. The housewife's parents allege that she was murdered by her in-laws who had been dissatisfied with the dowry she brought at the time of her wedding a year ago. However, the husband, Keshav Malik, a garment merchant in Chandni Chowk, and his father who were in the house at the time of the accident maintain, that Sushmita's sari caught fire when she was lighting a stove in the kitchen. Since the kitchen door was closed, they did not hear her cries for help. The police are questioning the women's relatives as well as neighbours and are reluctant to offer an opinion until the investigations are complete. At the insistence of Sushmita's parents, however, they have registered a case against her in-laws.

(iv) Accidents: Most accidents are reported on the basis of police bulletins or information supplied by police spokesmen. However, wherever possible the crime reporter must rush to the scene of a major accident to give authenticity to his story. For example, three members of a family–husband, wife and daughter–were killed on the spot when a speeding truck rammed into their car on the road to Indira Gandhi International Airport on Sunday morning. A fourth member of the family had a providential escape. According to the police, the truck driver lost control of the vehicle and swerved sharply to the right and hit the car coming from the opposite direction.

Those killed are Ramkishore Singh, a businessman of Agra, his wife, Sumitra Devi, and their daughter, Sapna. The second daughter, Tanuja, had a miraculous escape and suffered only minor bruises on her arms and legs. She was treated at the Safdarjung Hospital and allowed to go home. The truck has been seized by the police but the truck driver, Milkha Singh is absconding.

Example: Three members of a family - husband, wife and daughter - were killed on the spot when a speeding truck rammed into their car on the road to Indira Gandhi International Airport on Sunday morning. A fourth member of the family had a providential escape. According to the police, the truck driver lost control of the vehicle and swerved sharply to the right and hit the car coming from the opposite direction. Those killed are Ramkishore Singh, a businessman of Agra, his wife, Sumitra Devi, and their daughter, Sapna. The second daughter, Tanuja, had a miraculous escape and suffered only minor bruises on her arms and legs. She was treated at the Safdarjung Hospital and allowed to go home. The truck has been seized by the police but the truck driver, Milkha Singh is absconding.

Q8. Who is a reporter? Write essential qualities of a reporter.

Ans. A reporter is someone who investigates and reports news stories, either for a newspaper, website or broadcast news outlet.

Reporters are the key operators in any news organization—newspapers, wire agencies, newsmagazines, radio and television networks. They have also been called as the foot soldiers of the news world. A reporter is the primary source of news, the man who "brings it back alive". The reporter has the 'first crack' at the news. He decides how an event is to be presented. He is generally considered as the backbone of the news gathering operation.

The following are the basic qualities of a reporter or rather a good reporter:

(1) A Nose for News: A reporter must know what constitutes news. Without this he will not be able to gather news. A reporter's job of discovering the news has been simplified in one way and rendered difficult in another sense, in this age of information. While there are usual press notes on which news reports can be based, there are other sources of information on a variety of news event. The range of sources stretches from official spokesperson and press conferences to unidentified members of the public and the regular sources which one meets on the beat.

A reporter should be aware that quite often most of the material may just be advertisements or publicity matter in disguise. Thus, he must check the material and squeeze out the news that would interest the reader. A reporter is overwhelmed today by an ocean of facts but he has to rely on the reader's interest for guidance. Apart from this, a reporter most of the time has to cover routine matters such as press conferences and press notes. A reporter has also to report the speeches, declarations and announcements by VIPs, persons in authority, politicians and political parties.

Routine reporting should not prevent the reporter from looking for something unusual. A sharp sense of observation can help a reporter gather amusing sidelights of interest to the readers. Alertness will help a reporter to discover contradictions and problems while he is on his daily beat.

(2) Outgoing Nature: Introverts normally make poor reporters. Professional journalists are never armchair writers. A reporter has to meet people, make his acquaintance and win their confidence. It helps him to establish contacts, which in turn helps in writing well-investigated reports. This is the era of investigative reporting and readers are keenly interested to know what is going on behind the scenes. To get that kind of stories, a reporter has to be outgoing. He needs to develop an affable temperament and an easy-going nature.

(3) Ability to Establish Contacts and Develop Sources: A reporter has to be an outgoing person to establish contact and develop sources. Among the contacts, there may be some who can provide information to the reporter to serve their vested interests. Such information may comprise half-truths and even lies. So, a reporter must have other independent contacts through whom he can verify the information.

The Watergate scandal which shook the United States and the Nixon presidency was not exposed by any ace newsperson, but by two ordinary local reporters acting on a tip from an ordinary source.

The alertness and ability to pursue source help a reporter get the right lead. In the case of securities scam, the entire expose started with a source contacting Ms. Sucheta Dalal of the Times of India, Bombay, with an unconfirmed report about some activities in the state Bank of India. MsDalal, Assistant Business Editor of the paper, followed the lead provided by the source and got the story confirmed from reliable contacts bringing to light the stock scam of a staggering Rs. 6,000 crore involving stock broker Harshad Mehta and others.

(4) Ability to be an Unprejudiced Observer: The reporter must be an unprejudiced observer of events, one who presents the facts to the reader in a balanced, objective manner. It has been said that reporters mix comment with fact and so their reports are quite subjective. While reporters may have their own views on the subject of coverage, they should not allow personal opinions at any place in the copy. One must be able to throw light on unclear aspects if any, of the news event. At the same time, the news reporter must endeavour to write a report which is only a statement of facts. An observation or viewpoint, might occasionally creep in and one must be alert to such strips in straight news items.

To maintain balance and objectivity the first and foremost thing to do is to source the copy properly to assure the reader that what he is passing on as news, is not his opinion or some publicity matter is disguise. The sources must be quoted except when they want to remain anonymous. Even when he is not able to quote the sources, he must ensure that the story is balanced, by giving adequate coverage to all the sides of the subject.

In many cases, a reporter not only report the events but interpret them for the reader. But remember, interpretation does not mean backdoor editorialising. It is not an excuse for colouring the story with personal opinions.

(5) Clarity of Expression: For clarity of expression, a reporter needs to have command over the language. For clarity of expression, a reporter needs to have command over the language. A reporter may cover several complex and specialised subjects, such as science and technology, law and economics. His command over the language must be such that he can explain even the most complicated issues in single terms to any general reader. In addition to specialised subjects such as science and technology, even government press notes are written in complicated language, burying the news point. He must be able to simplify it and bring out the news point.

(6) Team Spirit: A reporter needs to have team spirit. He may have to work in a team. Many investigative stories are handled by a team of reporters. For example, the Bofors investigative stories in the Indian Express and other papers were based on reports from Geneva and Stockholm, besides, New Delhi. The securities scam investigations by the Times of India involved, Sucheta Dalal and R. Srinivasan, who posed as an investor and went to the State Bank officers in Bombay to confirm about the goings on in the bank. In the Statesman also some times stories are attributed to "The Statesman Insight Team".

A news reporter thus must be able to work as a member of such a team. He must pool his talents, sources and contacts into the team and work under a leader. A reporter may rise to head such a team also.

(7) Ability to cope with Pressure from Outside and Within the News Organisation: Reporters seeking to bring out scandals and exposures face pressure generally from people involved in such cases. People put pressure on journalists in the hope of preventing exposure.

The concerned journalist may also be bribed with attractive favours in return for silence on the matter.

As a newsperson, he may provide helpful or harmful exposure to persons holding important positions in his beat. Since many of them need publicity to perform their functions, they seek his out to provide them with the required exposure.

The pressure could be used to make change the news or "kill" a story. This constitutes censorship. Pressure could also be applied with the hope of inducing journalists to volunteer the change or omission which is then equal to self-censorship.

There are three ways of coping with pressure: fighting it, giving in, and anticipating the pressure and taking preventive measures. The first one is the most noble of the three options and history is full of shining examples of this category.

Running a newspaper is a business, apart from being a service. Thousands depend on it for a living. The reporters who generally brave powerful pressures are those who have the full support of their organisations or their professional colleagues backing them unitedly. But, still, they must have the strength of character to fight pressures that come in the form of inducements like lavish gifts, favours, etc. to influence their reporting.

Q9. Describe the important responsibilities of a reporter.

Or

Discuss the contribution of a responsible reporter to the news organisation.

Ans. Some of the important qualities essential for a reporter are given below:

- **Responsibility towards the News Organisation:** A reporter has been linked to a soldier on the field. Even as the quality of the soldiers on field determines to a large extent the quality of an army, a reporter's abilities and the way he discharge his duties as a reporter go a long way in determining the quality and reputation of his news organisation.

  As a reporter, he has to follow the character, style and policy of his newspaper or magazine or news agency. There are conservative papers which may prefer to stick to routine coverage, not bothering about investigation of scandals. In such newspapers, a reporter has to follow their policy even if it cramps his style. But in a news organisation with a more dynamic approach to news he must develop the skills of an investigator. Whatever he does as a reporter will affect the newspaper and its reputation. So, he must take pains to ensure accuracy and objectivity in his stories.

- **Responsibility towards the Sources:** Sources are sacred for a reporter. A reporter has to take great pains to establish his credibility to make them open up towards him. He will have to assure them that no harm will come to them, and if they so desire, he must keep their identity a secret. There have been instances in the United States of America and some other countries where reporters have defied court orders and gone to jail rather than reveal the sources. In 1960, an American magazine reporter alerted his edition that the ruler of a Middle East country was receiving large amounts of money from several governments for his personal use. But the reporter held back the story till 1977 as he felt that its publication would compromise his source. The matter became news only when the American Intelligence Agency (CIA, Files, made available to the press in 1977, contained the same information.

- **Responsibility towards the Reader and Society:** "Good faith with the reader is the foundation of all good journalism worthy of the name", says the code of ethics of the American Society of Newspaper Editors. As a news reporter's duty is to provide accurate, unbiased and objective information to the reader. Every effort must be made to ensure that the news is accurate, free from prejudices and that all sides of the news event are presented fairly.

  To maintain his credibility with the reader he should never accept things or favours or pursue any activity that might compromise his integrity.

  However, in these days, publicity seekers including those in private business, organise press conferences and conduct tours with attractive gifts and other incentives. While private firms depend mainly on advertising for publicity, they sometimes want their activities to be carried as news items since news carries greater credibility than advertisement. News reports are written by newspersons who are supposed to be independent and objective. While in these days of corporate and business journalism, it will be impossible to turn a blind eye to the activities of business houses, he must ensure that he is not exploited by them for selfish ends.

Dealing with Corporate News: A tremendous sense of responsibility is exercised by a reporter in the field of business and corporate journalism. With the proliferation of big companies including multinationals and their role in the liberalisation of the Indian economy, their activities form a major subject of public interest. But, it is a subject that must be handled with utmost care. On the one hand, a reporter may also have a risk of becoming a publicity agent for corporate houses and he may be risking people's investments and reputations. Anything reporting a news organisation could have its impact in terms of money and reputation.

Opinions about the newspaper industry have ranged from it being a mere business to an instrument of social change. Everything that a reporter writes could have its repercussions in the society. Even under normal circumstances, he has to exercise great care about what he writes.

Reporting Communal Conflicts: A reporter has to be careful when reporting in a communally sensitive country like India. This is because there are a host of religious and social diversities and several linguistic groups. It would be unbecoming to be partisan to a particular faith, linguistic or social group. As a reporter he will have to wield his pen with due respect for everyone. What may be considered correct by one group may be held wrong by another. Take the example of the Ramjanambhoomi Babri Masjid dispute at Ayodhya. Two concerned communities have a conflicting stand about the disputed structure. If he has been following the controversy in the papers, he would have found that the disputed structure is referred to neither as Ramjanambhoomi nor as Babri Masjid. It is referred either as the "Disputed site" or as the "controversial structure", or simply as the "Ramjanambhoomi-Babri Masjid site"

Apart from the Ayodhya dispute, the communal tension in the country has been aggravated by the Punjab and Kashmir problems. Reporters are extremely careful about reporting events of a communal nature.

Q10. What is the importance of interview in newsgathering? Describe the steps required for the preparation of an interview.

Or

Write a short note on 'off the Record'.

Ans. The importance of interview has been growing as a news gathering technique over the years. It is now seen more and more in news columns and at times because of interviews a newspaper scores over its rivals in news coverage.

The Importance of Preparing Oneself to Conduct an Interview: To conduct a meaningful interview both the reporter and for the person whom he plans to talk to, it is necessary that he does his home work right. An interview conducted after proper preparation would make a certain impact. It is said that to speak for five minutes over radio, a person must prepare himself at least for five hours. Thus, preparation is very important.

On the Record and Off the Record Interviews: Interviews can be on the record or off the record. On the record interviews are those whose contents can be attributed to the person interviewed. In this case, unless there is a prior agreement to use the whole of the interview verbatim, portions of the interview, that have some use for the reporter can be utilised and the rest discarded or canned for future use.

Off the record interviews are those in which the information is given, but the source is not to be identified by the interviewer. In such cases, the source identified is "a source in the Defence Ministry" or "a General Commanding a division" etc. In such cases it is normal to cross-check the facts from another source, since the man giving the information is not willing to stand up and be counted.

How to Prepare for an Interview: To know about the subject as completely as possible is the most important part of the interview. It could be a VIP, an important member from the bureaucracy, the art world or the corporate sector or just an ordinary citizen. The reporter should prepare himself by reading about the person. It is imperative for him to not only fully research the information he want from his subject, but also the person behind it. He should also have all the essential background information on the interviewee, e.g.his/her family, hobbies, interests. This will help him to build an instant rapport with the interviewee. It will enable him to get on with the job most comfortably. A reluctant interviewee only acts as an obstacle and foils the very purpose of the interviewer.

Steps required for the preparation of an interview are as follows:

(1) Research: It is most important to research on the subject matter. It could be a subject in which the reporter neither have any interest nor adequate knowledge. But once he is fully armed with the basic and important information acquired through books, newspapers, journals or magazine articles, he will be much more comfortable and should be successful in his venture.

For example, if he are required to interview a criminal lawyer, a policeman or an accused should have enough knowledge of criminal law - congnisable and non-cognisable offences, various Acts/Sections which govern the offences, and other legal provisions. This will help him extract the required information.

(2) Editing Interviews for Use: All journalists must remember two fundamental factors: First, all interviews are subject to editing. So there is no harm in culling more information than the reporter can use. The information that he need to buttress an arguments or to refute another or to make a point, can be used at the appropriate place. The rest can be stored for use to future.

Second, no statement made in the interview is allowed to be used out of context. If, for instance, a Government authority vehemently denies that human rights violations were made during a particular clash in Kashmir, one cannot quote him to create the impression that no human rights violations are made by security forces during any clashes. If the authority interviewed does not generalise it, the reporter or subeditor is debarred from generalising it.

(3) Strategy: It is important for the reporter to establish contact with the interviewee much in advance of the interview. The reporter can contact him directly – physical or through telephone. More often than not, where important interviewees are concerned, there is a channel he will have to go through. It could be the private secretary or the members of the family –referred to as the "protector of the interviewee."

So, the first thing to do is to establish a rapport with the protector. To get to your subject matter or the person, you must be able to play to the gallery to defeat all the obstacles imposed by the "protectors".

(4) What You Want from the Interview: The most important part of the preparation is to decide what the reporter want to get out of the interview. May be he wants substantiation of a fact discussed; Or the refutation of something; Or may be he wants the interview's views on some proposition he or someone else is making.

Here, an experienced journalist recalls for our benefits one such exciting interview that he had conducted some years ago.

In 1962 an International Invitation Table Tennis Tournament was held in Lucknow. Taking part were Victor Barua of England, FeremSido of Hungary who was among the first five in world Table Tennis. The cream of Indian Table Tennis was also there. The foreigners were lodged in Cartlon Hotel, the best of Lucknow those days, and the Indians in Capoor Hotel, the city's second best those days. Both were declared out of bounds for reporters because while the players played in the evening and until late at nights, they used to rest undisturbed during the day.

I was the Sports Editor of M.Calapati Rau's National Herald. The Sports Reporter did the spot reporting of the matches. I devised a way of getting past security to get to the players. A codeword prearranged with Meena Parande, who had been India's No. 1 player among women for seven years, was used by me to get to Meena's room in Capoor's at 11.30 a.m. one morning. As I knocked at and entered Meena's spacious room, in walked T. Thiruvengadam, K. Nagaraj and PappuHaldankar, the three top male players of the country.

I was clear in my mind that the objective was to find out about Meena's future plans. Though some of the questions might relate to Meena's past, background, experiences, etc., they were to be used only as ballast. The focus had to be on the future, since her past was already much written about and well known.

As I plied her with questions, she seemed unclear about her future plans. This put me on the alert. The plans of such high-ranking players are usually charted at least six months in advance. If this was not so, there must be something else in the offing. What was it?

Meena was 25 or 26. She had on top in India for seven years. By now it must not be very exciting to get one win after the other, to put it mildly. If one puts it bluntly, it should be quite boring.

I decided to probe from another side. Was she contemplating marriage? Considering that 25 or 26 is supposed to be a pretty ripe age for the marriage of Indian girls.

Neena gave me a look as if say, "How did you know?". Then she replied diplomatically, "Not before retiring from competitive table tennis."

Was she planning retirement?

Meena spoke the whole truth. What else? She had been on top of Indian Women's table tennis for seven years and had no more worlds to conquer. In International table tennis she was not in the top 50 among women, and 26 was not the age to go up. She could only go down. The wise thing was to retire now when she was at the peak.

"Now?" I asked incredulous as I realised I was on the trail of a scoop.

"Well", she said after a pause, "now or after the next Nationals", which were coming up in two months.

I asked some more probing questions. The male players echoed Meena's argument. All of them were going to retire. They had remained on top in India for years and had no hope of making good in the world arena. They were 27 or 29 and had to look forward to raising a family and carving a career for themselves. It was high time they retired. I had got the confirmation that I wanted. Coming back, I reported that India was losing the cream of its table tennis and quoted copiously from the interview. It was an all-India cream.

It is vital for an interviewer to decide what he wants out of the interview. It is not a fishing expedition in which you net whatever you get. It is a hunt where he goes after a target and get it.

The reporter has to keep his senses on full alert and the antenna unfurled to catch nuggets of news which have a knack of falling from the lips of the interviewee at the most unexpected moments.

(5) Preparing Yourself: It is important and essential, to make a deep study of the individual you plan to interview. Let us say that the person is particularly fond of dogs. When one go to interview her/him, it will be fatal to talk about how you abhor dogs or how they are dangerous. As interviewer, one cannot afford to convey your general wariness about the canine species - not verbally, not even through body language. The information you seek to extract from the person may have nothing whatsoever to do with dogs. Yet, the person may react by remaining uncommunicative through the rest of the interview if you start off on the wrong note. Paying attention to such minute, apparently insignificant matters really helps in conducting the interview smoothly.

(6) Physical Preparation: In the electronic media, there are two ways of interviewing: with the Prime Minister or the President, the setting would be as designed by the Public Relation Officer or the Principal Information Officer. If it is a television interview, then you need the following: (i) cameraman; (ii) sound recordist; (iii) lighting technician; and (iv the sound technician. The other way could be that the interview is to be held in a studio. In that case, you should adequately arrange the setting in the studio. For the radio studio interview, you would need a very good recording machine. You use a lip microphone which prevents extraneous sound from getting injected into the microphone. If the interview is only a part of what you are actually going to air, then it should be transcribed. Mark the important segments, and tailor the interview to the actual slot requirements with a suitable link to give necessary continuity. To do this, you would require an editor to do a proper cut and paste work of the tape.

Q11. List the skills that required for conducting an interview.

Ans. To get an interview can often be difficult because the interviewer is generally viewed with suspicion! To overcome this handicap, the interviewer has to be imaginative. The interviewer labours between two competing factors. One, the public has the right to know and the reporter is the tool employed to gather the information. Two, from the legal point of view nobody can be forced into talking and hence, the job can be tiresome and at times, very frustrating.

An interviewer or a reporter would in most cases, like to get information, facts and opinions from the interviewee. Therefore, it is very important that one's own participation in the interview is secondary.

There are number of skills and techniques have to be the reporters deployed to get feet inside before the door is slammed and he has his feet stuck up half way. The list is as follows:

- There is the direct approach: to telephone and tell the interviewee what he wants.
- The end round: A secretary in a business or government office will generally try and give the reporter the "brush-off" although the interviewee may be totally unaware of the secretary's action. He must recognise the go-between and try and make that person your friend. It is just a habit of the secretary to say that the boss has no time. The attempt of the interviewer/reporter should be to try and make the secretary/protector one's friend.
- When faced with repeated failure, find out the person's hide-out and with an overdose of apology, just barge in.
- Sit-in: It pays to just sit and wait till the subject of interview shows up in spite of secretaries and protectors saying that "the

boss has no time to see you". Take your lunch or dinner packet along with you to emphasize your determination.

- The appeal: As soon as get a glimpse of the reluctant interviewee, make an appeal as quickly and strongly as possible, e.g., "We have some information that you are to be shifted from your department/office" or something which will capture the attention of the object of your interview.
- Be courteous and polite: Tell the interviewee that there are two sides to every story, and we must yours. Thus, the reporter arouse the interviewee's curiosity and attention.

Q12. What are the Do's and Dont's for an interview?

Ans. Do's and Dont's for an interview are as follows:

- Be operational on time for the interview. This is very important. It shows the importance of the interviewee and that he has not been taken for granted. "To be 'operational" is a journalistic term described in the book Advances Journalism. In a nut shell, you must be ready right on time to start the interview. Arriving on time may be good in most cases, for one has to do things like setting up the camera, or recording devices before the interview. One should arrive 10-15 minutes before time in order to be operational on time.
- Outline your reasons for being there, unless you are working on something very sensitive. If you do not specify your reasons, it may create problems.
- Stan the interview with a broad question. This helps you to size up the person and also collect your thoughts. It also helps to receive information you may not have anticipated and to chart out your course of action-a correct direction that the interview should take.
- Do not interrupt until the interviewee has relaxed. Avoid making the interviewee uncomfortable at the outset. It would be of little value. An interviewee kept at complete ease can be most helpful.
- Let him speak at length on his favourite topic/achievement/ escapade/feat. You will get nuggets of information. The irrelevant facts can always be edited out. Be inquisitive, even

enthusiastic about his achievements. He will loosen up and be willing to come to the subject you want to discuss at length.

- Grunt and chuckle occasionally.
- Stick to your subject.
- Avoid commenting except to egg him on to talk more. Let the interviewee do most of the talking. This makes that person feel good and wise.
- Do not end the interview till you have the basics-how does he spell his name, official title, age, etc. Never ever assume that you know these things. Preferably get these details in advance from his staff and then get it confirmed by him.
- Be understanding. Do not be insensitive. Even a convict will remember that you were nice to him. Taking notes is a part of the interview. Also, make the interviewee feel important-often it is the interviewee who takes down notes. Relax and double check the contents. Keep the interviewee at ease.

Q13. Formulate your own strategy (course of action), according to the situation or person to conduct an interview. Also, discuss the tips for live interviews.

Ans. The reporter must not only be conversant with the subject matter of the interview but must also be a good conversationalist. All the important features of interpersonal communication come into play in an interview. In a face meeting, the stress is on both the language used in speech and the non-verbal body language. But, in a telephonic interview, the stress would be on the tone and inflexion given to the words. In this type of interview, it can be rather difficult to assess the intended meaning since the other person's actual expression in hidden from sight.

Preparing oneself to interview a personality, a celebrity or even the person-on-the-street is actually an on-going long-term process. This is because one must be a well-rounded interviewer, skilled in the art of handling a variety of topics and areas as also a range of idiosyncrasies that are inherent in people in general.

- **Your Part as the Interviewer:** As an interviewer the reporter should send and receive messages accurately. He should choose words that receiver will understand. He must avoid technical words and terms. Words should be very simple.

- **How to Generate Ideas for Your Interview:** Some interview are simply old wine in new bottles. Others seek to convey an innovation or idea that the interviewee has recently come up with. Yet other interviews are made out of the interviewer's ides(s): giving a new twist to an event, throwing new light on a discovery that had been accepted at face value, and such like. One must develop a keen sense of identifying material for use in an interview. One must also have the knack to read more into matters than is at first apparent: something like reading between the lines. That way, a much-interviewed persons may reveal a fresh side of the matter being discussed and perhaps also of his/her own personality hitherto hidden from public view.

Having a finely-tuned new-sense helps to generate ideas for interviews. It enables one to capture a glimpse of the extra-ordinary in the most 'ordinary' things and persons. It depends on the situation whether one comes upon a fresh insight during the interview by asking hard-hitting questions or by putting queries in a gentle manner. These are tactics that ought to be learnt by assessing and recognising the opportune time and place when it comes way. Alternately, the reporter could create the right atmosphere to make his interviewee reveal material which would form the basis for a good interview. In effect, the interviewer gives shape and direction to the interview, always allowing enough leeway for the unexpected utterance. One could then build carefully on what is sometimes said in such an offhand manner. The interviewer must, therefore, remain alert and latch on to every word that is said during the conversation. One can become adept in this technique only with practice.

Tips for Live Interviews: Following are some tips for live interview for radio or television:

- The speaker should be allowed to tell his story in his own way with due regard for the requirement of the medium
- The interviewer should keep in mind that the listeners want to hear him and they take the interviewer for granted.
- The speaker should feel completely comfortable.
- The interviewer should be strictly impartial, treating the rich and the poor, the famous and the humble with equal respect.

- The reporter should be sincere and never half-hearted or frivolous in his approach.
- Questions should be framed in such a way that they come naturally out of the speaker's narrative and are neither artificial spring-boards, nor impertinent instructions.
- The reporter should be friendly with the interviewee without being familiar.

Q14. What are the interviewing skills? Discuss how to establish rapport with the interviewee.

Ans. Advance preparation for the interview by way of well-thought out questions and a thorough consideration of approach is very helpful. One need not fear that the final outcome will sound stilted with no natural spontaneity. Usually the reverse is true. One will be able to pose the most appropriate questions when one is well-versed with the subject. The reporter should arrive on time for the interview. This will help keep the interviewee in good humor.

Taking Notes: Taking notes is an essential part of interviewing: the two cannot be separated. Some take down everything, even irrelevant and redundant remarks. Take down only what is important (and save time). However, that may not always be possible. People sometimes stop talking when they start writing. The reporter does not always know what is relevant until written it all down and reviewed it. He must train his mind to have a flawless recall. A wrong quote can be most embarrassing professionally. It costs he has credibility. Now-a-days, there is the help of a recorder. Take permission of the interviewee before using it.

- Write as fast as you can; knowing shorthand can be great help
- Keep hand and mind together, listen to key phrases; not the book references/citations. Verbatim quotes are especially valuable on touchy subject matters. A tape recorder helps you to review the interview in to. It is a must for a question and answer story. There are some disadvantages:

Always carry a note book. Never run out of tape or be faced with dead batteries. Remember to take down notes as well.

Off the Record: The reporter should remember honour-bound to respect and keep it secret in the best interest of journalism.

- Whenever you get a glimpse of the reluctant prospective interviewee passing within a running distance, make your appeal as quietly and dramatically as possible. "Oh... Mr./Mrs. so-and-so, we have information regarding...... which could prove sensational, Would you care to comment?"
- But be courteous: "We know there are two sides to every story. We want to hear yours."
- Some times nothing works better like an appeal to a person's sympathy. To asking a survivor of a tragedy, the reporter might explain how uncomfortable he feels asking question, and, how sorry he feels for him. But say, "could you please tell us what Chitra (the victim) was like? Do you have a picture?"

Good planning makes the interview successful and leaves happy memories for both – the interviewer and the interviewee.

Conducting an Interview: The reporter should try to know his subject—the interviewee. He should try to judge him whether the person is honest and what he is trying to hide. Through his eyes and mannerisms, the reporter can get reliable clues on how an interview is to be handled. The reporter must prepare a list of at least ten questions. But an interview rarely goes as planned. The interviewer thus requires a lot of instinct. If the reporter knows when and how to ask questions, he would be able to save an interview.

Establishing Rapport with the Interviewee: To build rapport with the interviewee, the reporter should do the following:

- In many small and big ways, try to make interviewee feel nice, cheerful and important.
- Outline the reasons for being there. Bring the interviewee up-to-date.
- Start with a board question. This helps the reporter to size the person and collect his thoughts. It also give him an opportunity to receive information which he may not have anticipated.
- Stick to the subject. Do not ramble or chit-chat. Neither is it advisable to beat around the bush. So go ahead and simply ask questions straight-away.
- Doodling or writing down a lot of useless matter in the reporter's notebook can be helpful. Those who have important

information to transmit, like to feel they are being recorded. Even so, try not to con his interviewee in this manner for too long! might be asked to show what has taken down! For all that, jotting down points helps him to prepare the transcription of the interview-session for publication.

- Listen. Listen. Listen. Not only does this make the interviewee feel good and wise, but it also helps you to control the interview. An interviewer might start speaking with good intentions and slowly digress. The reporter can bring him back to point.
- Be understanding. Nobody likes insensibility. The interviewee is often quite nervous while discussing his/her wrong doings, sin or tragedy. Help him/her to relax. If his mind goes blank, just say, "Excuse me. I forget where we were and what I need to ask".

2 SPECIALISED REPORTING

INTRODUCTION

Many news organizations assign journalists to cover specific areas either geographic or topical, known as "beats". Journalists get to know the territory and people who make up their beat and in many cases, they have to learn specialized vocabulary in order to understand their sources. Beats are rare in the smallest newsrooms, where every reporter is expected to cover every kind of story. But in larger news organizations, print and broadcast, journalists may have the opportunity to focus on a particular type of news. Some beats are traditional: government, police, courts and business for example. Others vary with the territory. Depending on a community's make-up, reporters might be assigned to cover the environment, or the elderly, or education as a beat. Although, specialised reporting deals with different areas as-Court Reporting, Legislature Reporting, Science Technology Reporting, Sports Reporting and Development Reporting.

Q1. What is court reporting? Briefly discuss the statement, "many courts few reporters".

Ans. Court reporting is an occupation wherein a person transcribes recorded or spoken speech into written words while in a legal setting. Those employed as court reporters are usually responsible for producing court hearing transcripts, depositions and other types of legal transcripts. A court reporter can also be referred to as a stenotype reporter, stenomask writer or a voice writer.

All newspapers even the big newspapers of India do not have the resources to cover all the courts of their main circulation area. The reason is there are too many courts. Newspapers neither have the time of the space to cover everything that happens in the courts. Newspapers cover only those stories which their readers are interested. A country governed by laws needs many courts, each with a different jurisdiction. The emphasis of the news media is on Criminal Courts, High Courts and the Supreme Court. The media are less interested in covering Civil Courts. One of the reason for this lack of interest may be that the Civil Courts are jammed with cases, the suits remain pending there for several years and it is assumed that in the mean time, members of the public would lose whatever interest they may have showed initially.

However, the media coverage of court stories is increasing these days. One of the reasons is that the courts are now getting more active in the fields of social justice. The number of public interest litigations is also increasing.

Q2. Who is a court reporter? What types of knowledge must for a new law reporter? Discuss.

Ans. A court reporter creates a written transcript in situations that require a word-for-word account of spoken words. Many of these situations involve judicial proceedings, but they can also involve closed-captioning and real-time translation services for those who have hearing disabilities. A court reporter has the ultimate responsibility to provide an accurate and complete record. A court reporter might create a transcript of depositions, meetings, speeches or other verbal conversations. In some locations, court reporters also assist judges and attorneys in areas of research or organisation. Some states require a court reporter to be a notary public, and some states require testing for state licensure. A newspaper which does not have a full time law reporter may send its regular staff correspondent to cover an important court story.

Must for a New Law Reporter: One would expect the Law reporter to be knowledgeable about legal matters. Here we will discuss the range and nature of information one must have at one's finger tips.

(1) Knowledge of Court Jurisdictions, Procedures and Hierarchy: A trainee journalist aiming to be a future Court Reporter must at first acquire some understanding of the court jurisdiction, its procedures and its hierarchy. At the apex, we have the Supreme Court of India. Then there are High courts, Sessions Courts, Magistrate Courts, etc. Also, there are Tribunals, for example, the Tribunal for Central Government Employees. If a reporter is acquainted with the jurisdiction of different courts, then one can easily locate the specific court for a particular matter. Similarly, if one is familiar with the hierarchy in the courts, one can easily guess where the appeal would be filed.

(2) At least knowledge of Some Legal Terms: For a court reporter, some basic knowledge of some of the most frequently used legal terms is a must. The following are some of the legal used quite often in the news reports.

Table 2.1

Adjournment Application	Request for more than for finding witnesses or important evidence or for other reasons.
Attachment Order	The court's authorisation to take and hold a person's property
Bail Bond	A security amount usually furnished to guarantee the appearance of an accused person in the court.
Change in Venue	Change of the place of trial.
Centorari	Writ from superior to inferior court requiring the records to be sent to the former for review.
Commutation	Reduction of sentence.
Concurrent Sentence	Court's decision that a convicted person serves only the longest of several jail terms imposed on him.

Contempt of Court	An offence against the court, punishable by a fine, or imprisonment or both.
Consent Decree	Court order to which the defendant has consented.
Decree Nisi	Final judgment to take effect some time in the future.
Double Jeopardy	Plea that the defendant has already been tried for the same offence.
Extradition	Process of returning a prisoner from one country to another.
Habeas Corpus	Judicial procedure requiring production of a detained person in court to inquire into the legality of the detention.
Mandamus	Court's command to an inferior court, or ordering a person to perform a public or statutory duty. Requiring someone to perform an act.
Pardon	Action of executive relieving criminal from sentence.
Parole	Release on promise of reappearance at regular intervals or on call.
Plaintiff	Party who initiates litigation.
Reprieve	Delay in execution of a sentence.
Proceedings held in Camera	Proceedings held privately, i.e. not in public.
Respondent	Party against whom an appeal has been taken
Proceedings Suo Moto	Proceedings launched by the court on its own.

Professional journalistic practice requires each technical term to be briefly explained when it is used in story for the first time. A legal term, not explained in the story, confuses the reader. Expect in professional or academic law journals, a news story must not be cluttered up with too many legal terms. The English language is predominantly used and for a reporter of non-English daily, some knowledge of English language will help.

(3) New Sources: New sources are very important in court reporting. Much of a reporter's success in the coverage of the courts depends on one's contacts and sources, and one's ability to gain access quickly to records. For a reporter the key person in a court is the clerk of the court. A court clerk prepares and keeps the records. He can make available copies of transcript for a fee. Court reporting involves diligent checking of recording. The presiding judge in a trail is seldom one's source. But a reporter should, as soon as possible, introduce oneself in person to the judge. A court reporter should also have good contacts with the lawyers working on a case and if possible with the respective parties. Where a case attracts much public attention, reporters may be under pressure from rival lawyers for a more favourable description of their individual positions. The reporter must then ensure impartial reportage in all fairness to the proceedings in court.

A court reporter should have adequate knowledge of different stages of civil criminal proceedings. One should also know where an appeal can lie from the court one is reporting. When a reporter is assigned to cover a major trail, the first thing one should make sure of is that one has a seat in the courtroom. One should also have adequate communication links with one's newspapers or news agency office. A reporter of a morning newspaper mostly does not face much problems in filing a court story, as one usually files the stories after the court retires for the day. However, for an afternoon paper or for services, the stories must be during the day, i.e., even sometimes when the court proceedings are on.

(4) Trial Coverage: While taking notes in a trial coverage the reporter needs to have a sixth sense. Guided by this news sense, one could begin to take notes of important dates. When a reporter misses an important testimony, one can always regain lost ground during the recess by consulting one's colleagues in the court, or the court stenographer.

(5) Writing with Quotes: In trial proceedings, wherever possible, the reporters must learn to quote the questions and answers or comments and remarks that arise in the course of the court's sittings. A story with quotes makes fascinating reading though sometimes, due to paucity of space, many comments may not be quoted in the news item.

Example (i): (Story without quotes) New Delhi, 3 February-A three judge Supreme Court bench comprising Chief Justice M.N. Venkatachalaiah and Justices P.B. Sawant and S.N. Singh, today, summoned three police officers of Etah district to appear before them on February 7. The three police officers including SSP S.N. Singh and SP Jamal Ashraff, have been directed to appear before the court to explain the alleged inaction of the UP police in pursuing prosecution of a man and his family members for selling off his wife into the flesh trade. The court ordered senior counsel Yogeshwar Prasad, who appeared for the state of Uttar Pradesh to produce tomorrow the records relating to the investigation by the police. Nasrin, the victim, was allegedly sold off to flesh traders by her in-laws and husband five years ago. Her mother ShakilaBano learnt in November last that her daughter had not vaishedmysteriously as claimed by her in-laws, but was actually in the red light district of Kasganj in Etah district ...

The same story with quotes, published in The Hindustan Times, New Delhi, 4 February 1994.

New Delhi, Feb. 3: The Supreme court today pulled up senior police officers of Etah district of Uttar Pradesh and asked them to appear-in-person before the court on Monday to explain their inaction in implementing the Court's order asking them to produce a 21-year old girl, who was sold off into flesh trade by her husband and his ' family. "As a result of police inaction, the girl, Nasrin alias Rani, has been destroyed totally and is a mental wreck and cannot even recognise her own mother", the Chief Justice, Mr. Justice M.N. Venkatzchaliah, who was heading a three-judge bench, observed. The Chief Justice, Mr. Justice Venkatachaliah, warned that if the officers were found guilty for not taking timely action on the Court orders they would be sentenced to substantive prison terms for contempt. The officer including one Senior Superintendent of Police, Superintendent of Police and one former Superintendent of Police, who has now been transferred to Ghazipur district were summoned to appear before a three judge bench comprising the Chief Justice, Mr. Justice Venkatachaliah, Mr. Justice P.B. Sawant and Mr. Justice S. Mohan. The UP police was also pulled up for not producing the records today...The Court rejected all excuses for delay, in producing the records as "red herrings" for their inaction.

Mr. Justice Mohan, another member of the bench, said that the very fact that the records had not been produced, despite the Apex Court orders, was proof of contempt of court. At this stage, Mr. Justice Venkatachaliah observed that the suppression of the records was deliberate...

The Chief Justice, Mr. Justice Venkatachaliah said that if this was the fate of the orders of the highest court one shudders to thinks of the plight of the public before the police. When the judges asked the counsel who had the custody of the records, he replied, "Stenographer of the SP". At this stage, the Chief Justice, Mr. Justice Venkatachaliah observed that "this is not the way to treat the highest court of the land. I know the mentality of the police from the way they come to court, enter courtrooms and sit in the court. They are an irresponsible lot". The counsel, Mr. Yogeshwar Prasad pointed out to the Court that the orders passed by the Court on December 15, 1993 asking the SP to produce the girl had reached his office on December 21, 1993. Since the SP was on leave since December 20, 1993 another officer was asked to carry out the orders of the court. As a result, the girl was produced before the Court on January 6, 1994. She was recovered by Rajasthan police from a village in Rajas than.

Q3. Discuss the precautions in writing court stories.

Or

What reporter can and can't report when crimes have been committed and cases go to court?

Ans. A reporter who writes court stories must be careful in avoiding any contempt of court. Sometimes, a reporter files the court story without comments and sometimes with one's own or someone else's comments.

Some illustrations of newspaper coverage of the courts:

Story without comments published in The Hindu, New Delhi, 19 January 1994:

New Delhi, Jan. 18.

The Supreme Court today, by its interim orders, stayed the execution of sentence of death imposed on Amrutlal Someshwar Joshi (accused petitioner) on charge of triple " murder" ....

The Chief Justice, Mr. M.N. Venkatachaliah, Mr. Justice S.C. Agarwal and Mr. Justice S.P. Bharucha, were on the Bench. The Bench made these orders during "mention time" on a request by Mr. K.K. Viswanathan, counsel for the accused petitioner for urgent orders of "stay" of execution of sentence of death of the accused pending the disposal of his Special Leave Petition (SLP) against his conviction and sentences of death by courts below.

Story with comments published in The Hindustan Times, New Delhi, 14 January 1994.

New Delhi, Jan. 13.

There was a mixed reaction by leaders of the three major political parties-the Congress, BJP and the Janata Dal to the Delhi High Court order quashing the Delhi government notification on holding elections for the Municipal Corporation of Delhi at present ...

Story with comments published in The Pioneer, New Delhi of 20 February 1994.

Even as one policeman after another presents himself before the apex court to receive what may be described as the harshest reprimand in recent history, serving and retired police officers feel that angry outbursts of judges and chief justices, however justified, will not ensure more efficient law enforcement ... Former Director General of the Border Security Force. K.F. Rustamji, believes the kind of language used by the court could have an adverse impact on the way in which the police will respond to situations in future ...

Story with comments published in The Hindustan Times, New Delhi, 14 January 1994.

New Delhi, Jan. 13 (HTC)

The High Court lawyers will strike work tomorrow to protest against what they call, violation of code of conduct by a high Court judge, Justice Sagar Chand Jain. Justice S.C. Jain vehemently denies all the allegations against him. The Bar's allegation is that Justice Jain was hearing a company case in which his son was a counsel and this was violative of a code of conduct for judges whereby a judge cannot and should not hear a case represented by his or her kith and kin.

The case in question was, in fact, represented by Mr. Huzefa Ahmadi, son of Justice Aziz Ahmadi of the Supreme Court. The Bar Association alleges that Mr. Ahmad! (Junior) was an associate of Mr. Pradeep Jain, Justice S.C. Jain's son: The Delhi High Court Bar Association, at an executive committee meeting this evening, decided to go on a day's strike to protest against this alleged violation of code of conduct for judges. Justice Jain, however, says he was not aware of the fact that his son's name was also in the vakalatnama filed by Mr. Muzefa Ahmadi. He said his son has never appeared in his court for this case. Justice Jain said as soon as he came to know about the fact that his son's name appeared in the vakalatnama, he ordered the case to be listed before another judge.

"It is blackmail", the judge said.

(1) Contempt of Court: The law relating to contempt of court can be braced from the Contempt of Court Act, 1971 and from various case laws. Contempt can be civil or criminal offences.

(2) Civil Contempt: Civil contempt means willful disobedience to any judgement, decree, direction, order or order process of a court, or willful breach of an undertaking given by a person to a court. There will be no civil contempt where is ignorance of the order of a court leading to unintentional breach.

(3) Criminal Contempt: Criminal contempt mainly means publication of any matter or the doing of any other act, which (i) scandalises or lowers the authority of any court; or (ii) prejudices or interferes with the due course of judicial proceedings.

(4) Scandalising The Court: Under the law, publication of matter which creates doubts about the ability or fairness of a judge of a court is prohibited. A new paper should not impute of improper motives to a judge. In 1971, in the case of Daphtary vs. Gupta, the Supreme Court decided that to express an opinion that a judge "toes the line" of another is contempt. Similarly, the expression the a judge pronounces his judgement under the influence of liquor or lure of wealth is also contempt. Casting defamatory allegations against a judge or judges, with or without reference to particular cases, is contempt because it creates distrust in the popular mind and shatters confidence of the general public in the judiciary. However, it should be made clear that the Contempt of Court Act, 1971, is basically designed to protect the judiciary from unwarranted allegations, and not to safeguard corrupt judges.

(5) Prejudicing Fair Trial: There may be various types of court reporting prejudicing fair trial. Contempt charges will be made against a newspaper on news TV channel (i) if a newspaper report deters a person from giving witness in a court; (ii) if the report offers threats or is written in abusive language compelling a party to discontinue the court proceedings; and (iii) if the report discusses the merits of a case pending in court.

In the famous Sheppard Case (1966), the judgement pronounced by the US court of reversed 12 years later on the basis of prejudicial publicity.

> Facts of the case were that Dr. Samuel Sheppard had served nearly ten years on his 1954 conviction of a charge of murdering his wife. Later in 1966 the court held that due to virulent publicity and a "carnival atmosphere" a fair trial was not possible. The U.S. media persons were warned that trials were not like elections, to be won through public meetings, radio, and newspapers. The media was also asked to show the increasingly prevalent habit of making unfair and prejudicial comments on pending trials.

The Dr. Samuel Sheppard case, as reported in Plain Dealer, Cleveland, U.S.A. (17 November 1966) gives an account of the reporter's experience of the proceedings in the court room:

Samuel H. Sheppard was found not guilty last night, in the 1954 slaying of his first wife Marilyn.

Sheppard gleefully slammed his hand down on the trial table after Common Pleas Judge Francis J. Talty read the verdict.

Sheppard had to be restrained in his joy by Defence Counsel F. Lee Bailey and co-Defence counsel Russel A. Serman.

"Sit down!" ordered Bailey, Sheppard sat down and burst into tears. A woman in the back row screamed, "Thank God"!

Other women could be heard screaming in the corridor outside the second-floor courtroom in the Cuyahoga Country Criminal Courts Building.

Sheppard's second wife. Aiane, covered her face and sobbed softly. She was sitting in the second row of the seats in the small courtroom jammed with nearly 60 spectators, 27 of them reporters.

As the jury was dismissed, Sheppard broke for the rear of the courtroom, thrusting a sheriff's deputy aside. "I'm going to see my wife", he said.

He leaned off the bar rail and embraced has wife, she threw her arms around him. "Oh, baby", he sobbed. "Oh, baby".

Leaping and pushing his way through the crowd that had amassed in the corridor, the former osteopathic neurosurgeon shouted, "He's my man!" and clasped the stocky Bailey around the neck.

Bailey, who had worked to have Sheppard freed in 1964 on a writ of habeas corpus, looked and beamed. This was the moment he had waited for—for 1,827 days, he had told the jury, every since he become interested in the celebrated Sheppard case in 1964...

Marilyn Sheppard, 31, died with more than 25 bonedeep wounds in her head. She was four months pregnant with her second child.

Asleep in the next room was the Sheppards' 7-year-old son, Chip, now a 19-year old freshman at Boston University. He testified in the current trial that he never awakened the night or morning of the murder.

Sheppard told authorities in 1954 that he was attacked and knocked out twice by one or more unknown assailants when he rushed to the rescue of his wife and later when he pursued a shadowy form to the beach behind the Lake Road home.

Sheppard was found guilty of second degree murder in 1954 after a 65-days trial, Sheppard served nearly ten years before he was released from prison on $10,000 bail by a US district court in 1964...

An area of legal control and constraint on free speech that is arguably more acceptable to and tolerated by journalists is that of contempt of court and court reporting restrictions. There is a general understanding and acknowledgement that in order for criminal investigations to be successful and courts to function without undue influence or impediment, some proceedings and aspects of those proceedings to require legal protection.

Recent years have, however, seen debate and contention focus on several aspects of contempt and court reporting laws.

First, there has been some judicial concession towards what has been a long-standing campaign to bring more openness into the family courts. While there is acknowledgement that the interests of children are best served by protecting them from unnecessary identification and reporting when it comes to legal proceedings, much of the criticism in relation to family proceedings has centred on the proceedings themselves and issues such as the credibility and integrity of expert witnesses and theories which courts have allowed to determine the fate and wellbeing of children and other vulnerable people. Allowing more scrutiny of proceedings while still preserving the anonymity rights of children is shining a long overdue light into the family courts.

Second, there have been some questionable instances of political interests being served through narrow and arguably inappropriate use of contempt laws to dissuade journalists from reporting on sensitive issues. When in the period between 2003 and 2006 journalists chose to question some of the decisions behind the political decision to wage war on Iraq and the treatment of prisoners there, there were several 'reminders' sent to news editors that they were subject to contempt laws.

Third, there is the uncertain and deeply unsatisfactory provision in Section 8 of the 1981 Contempt of Court Act that makes it an offence to 'obtain, disclose or solicit any particulars of statements made, opinions expressed, arguments or votes cast by members of a jury in the course of their deliberations in any legal proceedings'. While it is appropriate to shield the jury from influence while listening to a trial and arriving at their decision, it seems perverse that what is meant to be an open administration of justice criminally sanctions the discussion of cases and juries' decisions after the event. Fourth, there is the highly contentious issue of contempt of court law being able to be used to force journalist to reveal their sources. Section 10 of the 1981 Contempt of Court Act states that:

'No court may require a person to disclose, nor is any person guilty of contempt of court for refusing to disclose, the source of information contained in a publication for which he is responsible, unless it be established to the satisfaction of the court that disclosure is necessary in the interests of justice or national security or for the prevention of disorder or crime'.

The UK experience has been that when police or politicians play the national security or wider 'interests of justice' card, there has been considerable pressure on journalists to reveal sources. However, a recent ruling by the European Court of Human Rights serves as a useful reminder that at a European level (and as should be followed in the UK) suitable weight should be given to the freedom of expression provisions of Article 10 of ECHR and that prior to any judicial intervention in relation to journalists sources, there should be sufficient judicial investigation of the facts.

Q4. Discuss the main provisions of the Contempt of Court Act, 1971 and of some other status affecting court reporting.

Or

What do you understand by contempt of court? Explain its various types.

Ans. Section 5 of the Contempt of Court Act 1971 states that a person shall not be guilty of contempt of court for publishing any "fair comment" on the merits of any case which has been "heard and finally decided". Two questions arise. What is "fair comment" and what is meant by "heard and finally decided?"

- **Fair Comment:** "Fair comment" depends on the facts and circumstances of each case. There is no standard formula for this. To make a comment on the correctness of a judicial decision, whether on law or facts, is not contempt. In the same way, to print out inequality of sentences in two different cases of the same nature is also not contempt. However, if improper motives are imputed to the judge while commenting on the merits of a case, then the comment ceases to be fair. If it is that the verdict was arbitrary or the judge was incompetent to give the judgment is also contempt.
- **Heard and Finally Decided:** When a case is heard and finally-decided, a fair comment on the merits of a case can be decided. Until the period of limitation for filing appears has expired a case cannot be said to have been finally decided. If an appeal or revision of a case has been filed, the comments on the merits of the case should not be published until the appeal is finally decided.
- **Ignorance of Pendency:** If a reporter had no reasonable ground to assume that the proceedings were pending and publishes a court story interfering with the course of justice, he will not be guilty of contempt of court. Before the enactment of Contempt of Court Act, 1971, ignorance of pendency was not an excuse.
- **Fair and Accurate Report:** Section 4 of the Contempt of Court Act, 1971, states that fair and accurate report of the court proceedings is lawful. A report however will be contemptuous if it has been prohibited by the court and a newspaper publishes it.
- **Truth No Defence:** Truthfulness of a statement is a good defence in an action for libel, but it is no defence when it comes to contempt of court. This was the decision the Supreme Court

of India given in case of Perspective Publications vs. State of Maharashtra (1971).

- **Academic Writings:** A report written academically or any academic writings or on a point of law is not a contempt of court, just on the ground that the law discussed is at issue in a court.

Q5. Explain the terms often used in court stories.

Or

Mention the punishments and statutes which publications of court proceedings are restricted.

Ans. For contempt court, the maximum punishment is simple imprisonment of six months, or fine of two thousand rupees or both. If the accused apologises, the person may be discharged by the court without punishment. It is for the court to decide whether the apology is acceptable. An apology to be acceptable by the court, should generally be sincere, unconditional and without delay.

In the case of L. D. Jaikwal vs. State of UP (1984) the Supreme Court refused to accept an apology. The court imposed on the accused a sentence of one week simple imprisonment and a fine of five hundred rupees. The court ordered that in the event of failure to pay the fine he would undergo a further term of simple imprisonment of one week.

In the Suo Moto contempt proceedings against the newspaper Marathwada, Aurangabad Bench of Bombay High Court, comprising Justice V. V. Kamat and Justice Halbe accepted the apology tendered by the paper. The court observed that the contempt notice against the newspaper was being withdrawn, after the purpose of getting an apology was served.

Other Statutes Restricting Publications: Apart for the Contempt of Court Act, 1971, there are some other statutes which prohibit publication of court proceedings or any part thereof. For example:

- Section 228-A of the Indian Penal Code prohibits publications of names of victims of certain sexual crimes. The section also prohibits any other matter by which the identity of the victim could be known to the reader. Section 228-A was inserted in the IPC by an amendment made in 1983.

- Section 33 of the Special Marriage Act, 1954, requires that the proceedings under the Act should be held in camera if either party to the case wishes so, or if the court so directs.
- Similarly section 22(1) of the Hindu Marriage Act, 1955, requires that the proceedings under the Act should be held in camera if either party to the suit wishes so, or of the court thinks fit to do so. Section 22(2) of the Act prescribes punishment to be imposed on the person who prints or publishes proceedings without previous permission of the court.
- In the interest of the security of the State, Section 14 of the Official Secrets Act, 1923, empowers the court to hold the proceedings of a case or any part thereof in camera.
- Under the Monopolies and Restrictive Trade Practices Act, 1969, the commission may hear a case or any part thereof in camera.

Q6. Discuss the importance of Legislature Reporting and Basic Structure of the Parliament and the State Legislatures.

Or

Explain Legislature Reporting.

Ans. Importance of Legislature Reporting: Legislature reporting is an essential part of mass media function it is significant feature of Parliamentary democracy. Both people and the government benefited by legislature reporting. Parliament of a State Legislature, Vidhan Sabha and Vidhan Parishad, is called "legislature". Legislature" literally means – that which legislates or makes laws. It involves reporting day-to-day proceedings of these bodies. This task of reporting involves multifarious activities of legislatures, including the complex process of legislature and debates on subjects of public importance. Besides, the job also includes writing for the media about several other features that go to make Parliamentary proceedings.

Reporting the proceedings of a legislature is a highly responsible job. The knowledge of shorthand is advantageous for reporting parliament proceedings. Legislature reporting often involves taking copious notes of speeches made by ministers and members in both the Houses of Legislature. The exact quotes from what the Prime Minister or a Chief Minister or ministers or members, say in the legislatures are of crucial importance for the quality credibility of a reporter's dispatch. The reporter who knows shorthand has a clear advantage.

Basic Structure of the Parliament and the State Legislatures: Reporters covering proceedings of legislature should have an understanding of the basic structure of parliament or a state legislature. The Constitution of India provides for a bicameral Parliament consisting of the President and the two Houses–Lok Sabha (the House of the People) and Rajya Sabha (the Council of States). The Lok Sabha is composed of representatives of the people chosen by direct election. The maximum strength of this House now envisaged by the Constitution is 547. Out of these, up to 525 members come from the states, up to 20 members from the Union territories and not more than two members of the Anglo-Indian community to be nominated by the President of India if in his opinion that community is not adequately represented in the House.

Lok Sabha's term is five years from the date of its first meeting. During the operation of an emergency, the term may be extended for one year. Rajya Sabha consists of about 250 members. Of these, twelve are nominated by the President for their special knowledge or practical experience in such matters as literature, science, law, education, art and social service. The remaining seats are allocated to the various states and Union territories, roughly in proportion to their population. Each state is, however, represented by at least one member. The representatives of each state are elected by the members of the legislative assemblies of state in accordance with the system of proportional representation.

Legislative bodies at the Centre and States are great sources of news when in session. All the major decisions of the Government are taken in Parliament. Political parties also express their views on various issues in the Parliament. A reporter covering Parliament should know the rules and procedures of legislatures. There are moves and counter-moves by ruling and opposition parties which are grist to the newsperson's mill.

Parliament and state legislatures become great sources of news when in session. The Government makes all the major announcements in Parliament. Political news also comes from in and around the House in session as political parties express their views on various issues. The relative strength of the political parties is also tested on the floor of the House. There are moves and counter-moves by ruling and opposition parties which are grist to the newsperson's mill. As Parliament, there are some states which have a bicameral legislature – assembly and the council, i.e.Vidhan Sabha and Vidhan Parishad. The assembly in the state is the equivalent of the Lok Sabha and the Council is the equivalent of the Rajya Sabha. There are states which have only the Vidhan Sabha and no Vidhan Parishad. As a reporter covering Parliament, we should know the rules and procedures of legislatures. By and large, these are the same for the both the parliament and the state legislatures.

Q7. Describe the various features essentials of parliamentary proceedings.

Ans. The features essential for the parliamentary proceedings can be roughly listed on a normal day of proceedings, as under:

(1) Question Hour: Generally, the first hour of a sitting of Lok Sabha is devoted to Questions and that hour is called the Question Hour. It has a special significance in the proceedings of Parliament. Asking of questions is an inherent and unfettered parliamentary right of members. It is during the Question Hour that the members can ask questions on every aspect of administration and Governmental activity. Government policies in national as well as international spheres come into sharp focus as the members try to elicit pertinent information during the Question Hour. Questions are of three types: (i) Starred Question (ii) Unstarred Question (iii) Short Notice Question.

- **(i) Starred Questions:** A starred question is the one which a member desires an oral answer in the House. Other members can ask supplementary questions which are relevant to the main question. For this, a member will have to attract the attention of the presiding officer by raising his hand. Generally, the answer to the main question which is listed, is in written form with explanatory statement, wherever necessary. But supplementaries will have to be answered orally by the minister concerned.
- **(ii) Unstarred Questions:** In the case of "unstarred question" an oral answer is not given in the House. Supplementary questions are also not raised. To such a question, a written answer is deemed to have been laid on the "Table of the House" after the question hour by the minister to whom it is addressed. It is printed in the official report of the sitting of the House for which it is put down.

(iii) **Short Notice Questions:** A short notice question is one which relates to a matter of urgent public importance, and can be asked with the consent of the Minister concerned, at a shorter notice than the period of notice prescribed for an ordinary questions. Such Questions relate to a matter of urgent public importance. One day, 20 questions can be raised for oral answer, while as many 230 questions can be listed for written answers. A reporter should written questions. These questions are raised by the members from all states to they are late. A question can be very important for a reporter of regional daily newspaper thereof yield a great deal of information concerning various states and other Central government departments/ ministeries as the questions are asked by members belonging to each region of the country. The reporter who does the written questions has to carefully scan through all the answers to sift really newsy matter out of them.

It is through these questions, members express the grievances of the people of the region. Sometimes such questions led to an appointment of a commission, court of enquiry and important legislation if an issue of grave concern is raised. Thus, experienced reporters are entrusted with the task of pruning the questions and attending the question hour. The reporter should also remain alert during question hour as the minister concerned replies to questions quickly. If it is an important issue, a reporter can file the story immediately or can call the desk and gave the news. Later on the reporter can add background details and make it a good report.

For example, a few years ago, the government's signing of an agreement with Britain for the purchase of the aircraft carrier Hermes at a cost of 63 million was revealed in a written answer. With proper background, a lengthy, informative news story can be weaved out of this by an experienced reporter. Here is an example:

Express News Services

New Delhi, April 24.

The Government confirmed today that it had signed an agreement with Britain for the purchase of the aircraft carrier Hermes at a cost of 603 million pounds. The announcement was sneaked into unstarred questions in the Raiya Sabha in a style characteristic of the defence ministry on Wednesday. The defence ministry would not confirm or deny news reports from London that such a deal had been signed on April 19. The Indian people learnt fame major agreement to acquire a second aircraft carrier from British government officials. The minister of state of defence, Mr. Arun Singh, told Mr. Kalpna Rai, Mr. L. K. Advani, Mr. K. K. Birla. Mr. Suresh Kalmadi and Mr. D G. Prashant in written replies on Thursday that a memorandum of understanding was concluded on March 12 this year for the purchase of Hermes. The cost of the package was likely to be about 603 million inclusive of docking and refit spares, stores and services.

Mr. Singh said that a second aircraft camera was considered desirable in the light of the threat perceived. Hermes hay the facilities for operating Sea Harrier aircraft and Sea King helicopter which are already part of the Indian Navy's air arm. Hermes will he fully operational when it joins the Indian Navy and is expected to serve till the end of the century.

This not the first time that the defence ministry has sneaked a major announcement through the unstarred question in Parliament. It did this in the case of the purchase of eleven Sea Harrier last year at cost of 150 million.

Several weeks ago news reports appeared that the government had signed an agreement to buy Swedish 155 mm puns for the army. In this case also, news of the agreement was provided by the Swedish company concerned to a news agency.

Asked about it, the defence ministry spokesman would only say: "I have not been asked to deny it." No official announcement has been made on this so far.

The way the Hermes announcement was made-five days after agreement was actually signed-goes against the assurance the Prime Minister gave during his reply to the defence debate in the Lok Sabha.

Mr. Rajiv Gandhi said much had been made about the secrecy of defence contracts dealings and assessments. He said he had a feeling that documents were being over classified. "There is no intention at any time to keep the Parliament or the country in the dark about any details," he said but added that performance limitations and evaluation reports of equipment could not be revealed.

Members of Parliament have expressed concern about the secrecy surrounding such deals because they involve hundreds of crores of the tax payer's money and there have been a number of instances in the past of the defence ministry bungling these deals.

Thus, parliament questions cover all the ministries and give authentic information. They should be kept by the correspondent for future use as the) may provide leads to other stories. The questions provide basic data on almost all subjects that deal with the nation or state's economy and development and various other projects. This information can be analysed to yield many good stories.

(2) Papers Laid On Table: Papers laid on tables are official documents relating to various ministries and departments and are tabled by the ministers concerned. These papers often yield good stories. The documents may be annual reports of important government organisations, institutions of science & technology and other which have come into being by an act of parliament.

Also, the documents may include reports of the Public Accounts Committee (PAC), the committee on public undertaking, action taken reports of various ministries and so on. A reporter should carefully read the agenda paper of the House. It lists all the officials papers to be laid on the Table. As soon as they are tabled, the documents are made available to journalists by the secretariat of Lok Sabha or the Rajya Sabha, depending on which House the papers are tabled.

(3) Zero Hour: The term Zero hour in reference Indian Parliament means the time immediately following the question hour in both the houses of Parliament, i.e. Lok sabha, Rajya sabha. This session continues for one hour from 12.00 Noon till the house rose for lunch. Since this session starts at 12.00 Noon it is called as Zero hour. During the Zero hour the members are permitted to take up the issues of National importance and there is no specific rule in the Parliament regarding type of matters to be raised during the zero hour.

The Zero Hour follows immediately is the most challenging for a young reporter. For, this is the time when members belonging to various parties spring on their feet and try to draw the attention of the Chair to the issues they think important and need the Government's response. It becomes very difficult to pick up the works of the members as many speak at the same time. If the reporter concentrates on it, he can get something to file. However, the presiding officer would restore order and allow members to speak one after another.

In certain situation the presiding officer, however, would restore order and allow members to speak one after another. In some instances, the entire opposition may be united to put the government on the mat. Newspapers carry reports speaking of "pandemonium" or "bedlam" in the house over these issues. The reporter, with this notes and a fair background knowledge of the issues raised, will be able to write a good copy. It is also important for the reporter to be thorough with the morning newspapers, at least with the stories likely to figure in Parliament later in the day.

(4) Legislative Business: The general nature of the business of the legislature include of the following: Besides, the main legislative business of the house, which is introduction and passage of bills into laws, it also deals with the: financial business presentation, discussion and passage of the general and railway budgets. Voting on the various demands for grants followed by passing of Appropriation and Finance Bills; motions and resolutions brought forward by the government and private members; discussion on matters of urgent public importance; debate in the house on matters requiring decisions of the house; and publication of debates of the houses.

After a bill is discussed and passed by both the Houses, it goes for the Presidential assent. After the President nod, it becomes an act of Parliament. A bill, which is a legislative proposal, becomes an act after going through the following stages:

(i) **Introduction of the Bill:** The bill can be introduced in either House by a minister in charge of the subject of the Bill. While introducing the Bill, the minister explains the purpose and background of the Bill. Once the House, that is majority of members, gives leave to the minister for introduction, the Bill is deemed to have been introduced.

(ii) **General Discussion:** At the second stage, a general discussion takes place on the bill as whole followed by a clause by clause consideration of the bill. At this stage it is open to the House to decide to refer the bill to a select committee of the House or a joint committee of the two Houses. The committee then gives a close and detailed scrutiny clause-by-clause and makes such amendments therein as it deems necessary.

(iii) **Voting:** When all the clauses and schedules of the bill have been considered and voted upon by the House, the minister in charge moves that the bill be passed. Generally, a bill is passed by a voice vote. But on other occasions, a division may take place and the bill may be passed or rejected by a majority of the members present and voting.

(iv) **Constitution Amendment Bill:** A constitution amendment bill, at times, requires the support of the majority of the total membership of the House and two-thirds of the members actually present and voting.

Q8. Write short notes on the following:

(i) Call Attention Motion

Ans. The procedure of Calling Attention to Matters of urgent public importance was for the first time introduced in 1963 in the Punjab Legislative Council. It had been used more frequently than the Short-Duration.

It is the right of every member (with prior consent of the Speaker or the Chairman) to call for the attention of a minister on a matter of urgent public importance. This unique Indian concept of 'Calling Attention' allows members to highlights failure or inadequate action of the government on an important matter of public importance. This procedural device is similar to an adjournment motion without its censure aspect. The minister is allowed to make a brief statement or request a later date for making a statement.

(ii) No-Confidence Motion

Ans. The changing political composition of Parliament has led to a new procedure known as the Motion of Confidence in the Council of Ministers. This practice has evolved in recent times and takes place whenever no single political party is in a position to command the majority of the House. The procedure followed is as follows: a one-line motion under Rule 184 "that this House expresses its confidence in the Council of Ministers" is moved by the Prime Minister on the direction of the President. The Council of Ministers remains in office as long as it enjoys the confidence of the Lok Sabha. If the Lok Sabha expresses a lack of confidence in the Council of Ministers, the Government is constitutionally bound to resign. In order to ascertain the confidence, the rules provide for moving a motion to this effect, which is called a Confidence motion. A motion of No-confidence, once admitted, has to be taken up within 10 days of the leave being granted. Rajya Sabha is not empowered to entertain a motion of No-Confidence.

(iii) Special Debates

Ans. Special debate on a subject of national importance is allowed by the Speaker at times. Almost each member of the House is given a chance to speak in the debate.

(iv) Adjournment Motion

Ans. Adjournment Motion is the procedure for adjournment of the business of the house for the purpose of discussing a matter of urgent public importance, which can be moved with the consent of the Speaker. The Adjournment Motion, if admitted, leads to setting aside of the normal business of the House for discussing the matter mentioned in the Motion. To be in order, an adjournment motion must raise a matter of sufficient public importance to warrant interruption of normal business of the House and the question of public importance is decided on merit in each individual case. The purpose of an Adjournment Motion is to take the Government to task for a recent act of omission or commission having serious consequences. Its adoption is regarded as a sort of censure of the Government.

(v) Budget

Ans. Budget is the annual financial statement presented before both the Houses. It includes the estimated receipts and expenditure of the government in respect of the forthcoming financial year. The finance bill is introduced in the Lok Sabha immediately after the presentation of the budget. It seeks to give effect to the government's taxation proposals.

Q9. What do you understand by Parliamentary Privilege? Write the significance of Parliamentary Privilege.

Ans. According to Article 361-A of the Constitution of India protects publication of proceedings of Parliament and state legislatures from any civil and criminal action. No person commits any civil or criminal offence, if he publishes substantially true reports of the proceedings of a House. However, if the publication has been done with malice, the protection conferred by Article 361-A does not apply. Publication of the expurgeal portion of the proceedings of a House, is breach of its privilege. Similarly, publication of those proceedings is disallowed which are held in camera. Article 361-A was inserted in the Constitution in 1977. Before this, a substantial and true report of the proceedings of either House of Parliament was protected by Parliamentary Proceedings (Protection of Publication) Act 1956, popularly known as Firoze Gandhi Act. However, during the period of internal emergency, the Act was repealed. Later the emergency Article 361-A was inserted through a Constitution Amendment bill. Article 361-A has wider scope than what the Firoze Gandhi Act had. Article 361-A covers publication of proceedings of Parliament as well as that of the state legislature, whereas Firoze Gandhi Act covered only the House of Parliament.

Reporting the legislature's proceedings by the media is extremely useful for the common people in a democratic set-up. For, it is through the day-to-day reporting of the legislature's activities that electorates perceive as to what these elected representatives are doing in Parliament and other legislatures. Journalist, therefore, have to be on the constant look out for publishing important decisions taken or not taken in these Houses. In doing so, journalists are sometimes likely to error on the wrong side of the law. Members of the legislatures have a large number of rights, privileges and immunities which protect them against attacks by people and organisations including the media. Thus, with a view to ensuring that media do not cast aspersions on their conduct or adversely comment on their report in a House, a number of common laws have been provided. These laws govern the powers and privileges of legislatures in so far as these common journalists' work may interfere with the right to the freedom of the press or reporters. Though Indian parliament or legislatures have so far not fully codified their rights and privileges, they generally follow the conventions and traditions of the British House of Commons. Many of these Parliamentary practices are described in the "Parliamentary Practice" by May.

According to Durga Das Basu, a journalist may encounter privileges of parliament in a number of ways:

- by violating any of the privileges of Parliament, e.g., relating to publication of proceedings;
- by violating any of the rules of procedure made by a house of legislature in exercise of the power conferred by Articles 118

and 208 of the Constitution of India, e.g., relating to admission and withdrawal of strangers;

- by publishing comments or any other statements which undermine the dignity of the house or the confidence of the public in the legislature, and are, accordingly punishable by parliament as contempt of parliament, which is analogous to the power of a court of record, to punish for "Contempt of Court."

The representative of the press are generally provided facilities to cover the proceedings of legislature from the press gallery by issuing an accreditation card to press persons. The accreditation card can be withdrawn by the Speaker without assigning any reason. Normally, a card is withdrawn, if a journalist is found to be "misrepresenting proceedings of the house in the press, or publication or of any matter not intended for the public, or casting aspersions against the Speaker."

The reporters should however study parliamentary privileges and Article 361-A of the Constitution of India to safeguard themselves against any default that may occur in reporting proceedings of a legislature.

Q10. Discuss various types of committees of legislature parliament.

Ans. A legislature parliament has two kinds of committees:

- **Adhoc Committees:** These committees which are for a particular purpose or function and only for that time-span may be appointed by the House or by the Speaker either by himself or on the recommendations of a Parliamentary Committee. Examples are: Five Year Plan Committees, Committees appointed on the Conduct of Members, for Amendment of Election Law (1970), Committee on the Use of language etc.

  Select or Joint Committees on Bills are also ad hoc Committees and are examples of Committees appointed by the House. Usually a Motion for reference to a Select Committee also specifics the names of Members for the Committee. In case of Government Bill the Minister in charge of the Bill is appointed as Member of the Committee.

  The Speaker appoints Chairmen of all Standing Committees.

  In case of the Committee on Public Accounts, the Membership is in proportion to different parties and groups in the House so that they are represented in proportion to their respective strength in the House. As per a well-settled British Convention, the Chairman of the Committee on Public Accounts ought to be from the main opposition parties or groups and in a rotating manner. However, this convention has not been established or strictly followed in India.

In the Indian Parliament there is no Committee of the Whole House and the Mace on the table of the Speaker (much relevant for the said Committee) is also absent.

- **Parliamentary Committees:** Parliamentary committees are regular committees, but are reconstituted from time to time. These are: business advisory committee, committee on petitions, privileges committee, committee on welfare of scheduled castes and scheduled tribes, rules committee, etc.

  However, there are yet other kinds of committees which function as parliament's "Watch Dogs" over the executive. These are: committee on subordinate legislation, the committee on government assurances, the estimates committee, the public account committee, and the committee on public undertakings.

Composition and Functions of the Committees: These committees appointed by the legislature play an important part in exercising a check over governmental expenditure and in the general discharge of the public functions. It is, therefore, necessary for those reporting legislative proceedings to keep track of the reports these committee submit, on the task they are entrusted with, by the house. The reports and the functioning of these committees, also make good news. It is useful for reporters to know the composition and the discussions among the members of these committees, for they also make good news quite often. Moreover, often the business transacted by these committees adds up to the overall legislature reporting by a correspondent.

Q11. Discuss those points that would help in brushing up knowledge of science to become a science reporter.

Ans. Reporters with science background and who have interest in science and technology should be specifically assigned the task of science and technology reporting. Of course, any one can become science reporter if he brushes up his knowledge on the subject and goes on adding to it.

(1) Recapitulate School and College Science Studies: Recapitulation means going over again or revising the main points relates to science –

laws, theories, principles etc. All science reporters must have a basic knowledge of the elementary principles of science. A knowledge of scientific vocabulary is necessary. That does not mean only science graduates can report happenings in science. In a way, such education helps, but science education at school is broad-based and can be built upon. All students are given the basics of science and mathematics at school. It is possible to go over what we learnt in our early years at school memory has it all stored for re-call. A novice reporter going for science beat should brush up his science knowledge. Ph.D. in a science does not necessarily make one a good science reporter. With a scientific temper, a reporter will do better in science and technology beat.

A reporter with a scientific mind will never accept blindly If someone says "rainfall has diminished because of the sinful activities of humans". Instead we will try to find out what is "sinful activities". It may be deforestation, water and air pollution, heating up of the atmosphere by industrial activities. These activities can lead to climatic change, including less rainfall in some places.

(2) Tips on Science Communication Awareness: A science reporter must have the curiosity to know the latest happenings in the field of science and technology. The moment that reporter has learnt enough about a particular happening, he can write it as a report for publication. A science reporter's work involves three stages:

(i) search and research
(ii) understanding it completely and
(iii) writing it in a simple style to make your readers know what you have learnt.

The best way to develop science communication awareness is by reading good popular science books and journals. Also, watch popular science programmes on Indian and foreign television channels. He can ask himself why he liked a particular report. He will realise that the particular report appealed to him not necessarily because it brought out some startling facts, but because of its clarity of style so that the lay person can understand it.

(3) Checking Facts through Reference: There is no scope for factual errors, half-truths, bluff, exaggeration and hoax in science and also in science reporting. Scientific truths and technological facts are verifiable. In the modern world, reference books and computerised knowledge banks are there to verify your findings. When the reporter hears about a discovery by an individual or an institution and if it has an element of half-truth or exaggeration in it, he must verify it from different sources. Science and Technology reporting widens mental horizon of the reporter. A reporter may be working on one story, his mind works itself to show the way to another story. Also, a reporter who verifies facts as a matter of habit will earn the reputation of being credible.

(4) Verification through Interviewing those who Know: A science reporter should always keep a list of scientists and technologists of merit, living in the city or town where he is functioning as a reporter. A reporter should maintain good contacts with all these experts. In case the reporter visits a scientific institution, he should meet the PR or Information Officer and get the list of the scientists. He can also meet scientists there if he gets the opportunity.

This way, the reporter can develop his contacts. The reporter should ensure that he approaches the scientists whose area of study and research is appropriate to the theme of his story. When reaching to an appointment, a reporter should be punctual. He should get a list of questions ready with him. He can record the interview. Before recording it, he must ask and take the permission of the interviewee. Even if the reporter records the interview, he should take note of important points during the interview. Also, he must get a photograph of the scientist expert interviewed.

(5) Personal Glossary of Common Science-Technology Terms and Phrases: A science reporter, like all reporters is hard-pressed for time. Every writer needs a good dictionary on his writing desk. As a science reporter, he will often be faced with technical terms. Scientists and technologists, and indeed all specialists are fond of, or used to, speaking in their own technical language, or scientific jargon. While taking down notes, he may not be able to translate these into common language. Therefore, he can prepare and keep his own glossary of commonly used technical terms. Arrange the words and phrases in alphabetical order. He can prepare such a reference material by working in the reference section of a science-technology library, or a good general library. He should keep updating the list as he progresses in his reporting career. If he has a glossary of technical terms handy, his report will make smooth reading. Newspaper offices do have reference libraries. But do not depend entirely on them. They have too many customers. The reporter should try to submit the reporter before time keeping in mind the deadline.

Q12. List the sources from which news stories on science and technology can be obtained.

Ans. A science reporter should not wait for news to drop on his desk. He must go and look for it. The reporter should always remain alert. He must do regular checking. He should also develop friendly relations with the information officers of the institutions. There will be different types of the institutions. There will be different types of scientific institutions which a reporter may use as his source.

A reporter should not think that institutions which bear "science" or "technology" in their names are the only sources of science-technology news, sources can be any government department, institution or organization. There are government departments dealing with public health, water supply, electricity, telecommunication, construction, transportation, etc., they have all applied science in multiple ways.

A reporter can find technological news from government offices and banks which may be going in for computerization or industries which may be going in for new technologies and the real estate business which may be opting for taller and taller buildings.

If the reporter is alert, he can find news everywhere. Suppose in the local paper there was a headline, "Sitapur to have a 20-storey building - tallest in the district". This is a general report sourced from a construction company, or from the town planners. People of Sitapur are happy that their own town will have a 20-storey building. People of neighbouring town of Jaipur will wonder and fell jealous why their own cannot have a 20-storey building.

A science reporter can look at the story from other angles. He can go to the town-planning department and ask whether such a tall building is appropriate in Sitapur. What about water supply and electricity? Is it feasible?

The reporter can meet the architect of the building and talk to him. He can meet the building contractor and ask him about his experience in building tall structures. What about fire safety? What about the foundation? What about structural stress analysis?

The report may be instrumental in creating scientific temper among the people of Sitapur. Press conferences, press handouts and policy announcements by ministers are the only sources of news for a science reporter. Events and phenomena in any area of the subject throw up news stories. For example, population densities, epidemics, soil salinity, good and bad water management, observation of fauna and flora of the region and non-conventional energy sources are all sources of news.

Q13. Discuss the role of institutions of research and development for a science reporter.

Ans. As a reporter covering science and technology in India, he must have a comprehensive knowledge of the institutions of research and development in the country. India has the world's third largest reservoir of technical and scientific manpower. India has also built up one of the world's largest network of R&D facilities. In the present liberalised industrial and economic climate, these laboratories and research stations will set new goals and work towards achieving them. They will be a major source of science-technology news.

The Department of Science and Technology (DST) looks after the policy planning and administrative details of the largest chain of national laboratories. These labs come under the Council of Scientific and Industrial Research (CSIR).

The premier national laboratories under the CSIR include the National Physical Laboratory, New Delhi; National Chemical Laboratory, Pune; Central Drug Research Institute, Lucknow; Central Glass Research Institute, Dhanbad; Indian Institute of Oceanography, Goa; and Electrochemical Laboratory, Karaikudi. The CSIR headquarters at Rafi Marg, New Delhi-1 is a great source for a science reporter with all the information one may enquire about in a professional capacity.

The Indian Council of Medical Research, under the Union Ministry of Health and Family Welfare, runs a major chain of research laboratories. There is also Research Development Service Organization under the Railway Board. Every university has research programmes going on in their post-graduate departments of Physics, Chemistry, Geology, Biology, Medicine, Agriculture and Engineering.

Atomic Energy and Space are two of the areas where India can boast of frontier research and development. The atomic power stations and rocket development and satellite launching events, capture the headlines. The Bhabha Atomic Research Centre and the Tata Institute of Fundamental Research, both in Bombay, and research facilities linked with these and scattered over the country, have been doing multi-disciplinary, high technology R&D which have success stories to be written about. The Indian Space Research Organization (ISRO) has done outstanding R&D work at its various facilities, which speak volumes for the caliber of its scientists. Both the work and the scientists are news. Technical departments under other central ministries too have their research programmes under specialised agencies. Department of Agriculture does a wide range of crop research through the laboratories and research stations of the Indian Council of Agricultural Research (ICAR).

The Indian Institutes of Technology (IITs) also conduct a considerable frontier research. The Indian Institute of Science at Bangalore is rated among the world's top basic science research organisation. So there is a vast opportunity for a science reporter.

Q14. Discuss the biographical knowledge of three categories of scientists and technologists which must be in reporter's mind.

Ans. A science reporter must have a cursory knowledge of outstanding scientists and technologists because leading names make leading headlines. A reporter may encounter with a leading scientist who may be on a visit to the town where the working. Editor may ask the reporter to interview the person. The reporter may be covering a lecture, which he delivers at a local function. If the reporter is familiar with the highlights of that person's life, the news reader's interest. A science reporter must have biographical knowledge of three categories of scientists and technologists:

- Outstanding men of science of the past who made path-breaking, or epoc-making inventions. Their work is globally recognised. Reference to them can be found in an encyclopaedia of science, or even in general knowledge books. In day to day reporting, such names may not and cannot figure. But the science reporter's knowledge should extend beyond the usual current affairs.
- India's outstanding scientists and technologies of the past – say, since the renaissance. Here will figure name like C.V. Raman, Jagadish Chandra Bose, M.S. Krishnan, K.S. Krishnan, Homi Bhabha, MeghnadSaha, S.S Bhatnagar, Vikram Sarabhai, etc. They have tremendous significance because their contributions

led to India's present-day achievements in science and technology. Their connections and interactions with India's first Prime Minister, Pandit Jawaharlal Nehru, enabled the latter to lay the foundations of independent India's science-technology progress. If India is in a position to import, adapt and cope and with the very latest technologies, it is because of the institution building efforts of the Nehru-Bhabha-Bhatnagar team.

- India has scores of living world-class scientists and technologies. They are to be found in every discipline and sphere of science and technology. It is beyond the scope of this unit to list them.

Q15. Explain how Science-Technology induced Development and Environment.

Ans. In modern times, much is said and written about the human environment, both physical and social. The print and electronic media put out almost a daily dose of news and features about the environment. Many people wave these away as being a fashion or a fad. For others, the word "environment" is almost like a mantra. However, a science reporter, must be cautious not to fall into such traps. That means, he must have a deeper understanding of the environment. The deeper his understanding of the environment, the higher would be his scientific temper.

Our life is much connected with the environment which is complex and delicate, too. Look from any angle of human development, and the fast changing environment condition will become evident to us.

Development has its impact on environment. He just look around our house and see the change in the last one decade. Tall buildings have come up all around. Very little sunlight enters our house. There is the stench of garbage in the air. The water supply comes only for an hour in the morning and an hour in the evening. The tree from which we used to hear the chirping of birds is no more there. The roads and lanes are littered with cars, people and garbage.

If we think about all the technology inputs in our home and neighbourhood. People have vacuum cleaner, washing machines, micro woven, air-conditioner, refrigerators, ipad and iphone and many other things.

There is also another type of impact of development in rural areas. People from usual areas are migrating to urban areas. There is rural underdevelopment. Migration of people to urban areas is resulting in the growth of slums in towns and cities. Similarly, development is leading to the rampant tree-falling for fuel and timber, and for agriculture, which leads to deforestation, top soil erosion, floods, reduced rainfall and desertification.

The science reporter can play an important role. A young reporter may not cover big conventions and conferences, there will always be lots of stories to cover. One story will lead to another if the reporter has a keen scientific temper and alert.

Q16. Briefly discuss the impact of science and technology on social attitudes.

Ans. Terrific change is the age of science. Technology, as applied science, has infused rapid movement in every conceivable human activity. Whether it is transportation or communication, construction or manufacture, exploitation of natural resources or polluting the environment, speed is the main phenomenon. Speed in production and consumption has come to be taken as the criterion of progress. This has led to competitiveness in acquisition of goods and services. Individuals, societies and nations are caught up in the acquisitive attitude which manifests itself in norms and policies. The result is social distortions, intra-group competition and conflicts.

A science reporter is not just a collector of spot information. Of course, he has to do as a daily routine. But, while doing that, his social perceptions too will get sharpened. He will observe the holistic picture of the pros and cons of heightened, technology-infused change on society. Reports of such developments make societies take stock of themselves. Such reports help policy makers take corrective measures. If a science-technology reporter wants to study the electronics industry, he may start with entertainment electronics. Then, he will learn about professional electronics, then, information technology. But then, he would have had glimpses of computerisation and automation. By the time he begin to have a complete view of the electronics industry, the whole technology would have undergone rapid changes. He must keep pace with technology updates.

Satellite communication has revolutionalised the world. Television channels have gone global. Print technology has changed. Now news travels as fast as light. The concept of global village is a fast materializing reality. Now it is necessary to have a global view. However, good reporting is not done from the global viewpoint. A reporter should see the happenings at local regional, national and international levels. While writing a report, the reporter should always keep the reader in mind. While reporting a specific development in technology, if he provides the social implication of its application within a time frame, the reader will take interest.

Q17. Discuss the language that is used in Science-Technology Reporting for Popular Appeal.

Ans. In science reporting, the language should be simple and understandable to common readers. News writing must be short and precise. Science reporting should be even more precise. Ideas and images in science communication should flow in logical progression. The written language must be like a precision instrument if it is to register the meanings in the minds of those in a hurry.

The English Language has been accepted as the global language of the science-technology era, it is because of three reasons:

- It has had a global spread
- Since Newton's time, major developments in science and technology have taken place in the English speaking world. Certainly there have been developments in areas speaking other languages. Nonetheless, there is a chance that the people may be acquainted with the English language and they may have published their discoveries and inventions in English.
- The English language is a changing language. It keeps in tune with the changing times. While keeping the basic standards of grammar, it is amenable to improvisations.

The English language is today considered as the window to the science-technology information of the world. Even the non-English science-technology intensive areas of Europe, the Russian Commonwealth of Independent States and Japan, are introducing English language studies in a big way. Therefore, no matter in which language the reporter proposes to write as a science-technology reporter, a keen knowledge of the English language is also a must for him.

Words, Sentences and Readability: Words denote images. Nouns evoke images of objects, subjects, actions etc. Verbs work the Nouns. All other forms of words are accessories to the chains of words, which we call sentences. There are tested patterns of constructing newspaper stories. The opening sentences must say the important point of the news. The first sentences, on its own, or the first two or three sentences should give the gist of the story. The paragraphs must be small. Fifty-to-sixty word paragraphs are considered to be ideal in news writing. Remember, the story must move on from sentence to sentence, and paragraph to paragraph. Otherwise, the reader will feel the jerk. Readers have a tendency to abandon a news item at the point where it begins to jerk or waver, unless, of course, they have a specific and special interest in it.

Report Structure: The science-technology news report structure is not different from that of any other news report. A good beginning (intro), followed by the more important news points at the top of the story. That is the accepted pattern. All the five Ws and one H – who, what, when, where, why and how – need not be cluttered in the intro. But these elements of beginning a news story must appear at the top. Nothing is ever printed without being edited. Every report that is produced by the reporter goes through the creativity of editors, particularly news editors and sub-editors. If it is badly is badly written, no one on the editorial desk has the time or inclination to rewrite it. Science-technology news reports are almost never rewritten, because nobody wants to be accused of having tempered with its precision.

Human Interest: Readers are interested in reading something which concerns them directly – young or old, man or woman, you or yours. If the science-technology story says something which people are interested in, just make it felt. If it is about a fuel-saving device, just start: "An automobile user can now save 20 per cent of his fuel cost by opting for the 'so and so' engine system, claimed the makers of etc. etc". The reporter should make them (readers) realise that he is their reporter. Do not fall for advertisement techniques of selling. Instead, seek to be the best source of information for the readers.

Avoiding Exaggeration and Sensationalism: Exaggeration and sensationalism catch the attention of the reader. But science-technology facts simply cannot hold exaggerations. If a discovery, invention, or improvisation has an element of sensation, the reporter should not be inhibited in including some of the sensational in his story. But do not make an invention look like something the world has been waiting for, when it is just an improvement one something that already existed.

Sensationalism and exaggeration can only do harm to the publication and to the credibility of a reporter. A reporter whose credibility is repeatedly doubted, can never grow professionally. Just like the scientist, a science reporter also should be a seeker of truth. Like a technologist, a technology reporter too should be one who believes in precision and in updating knowledge.

Importance of Rewriting: A sentence, a paragraph or a piece of writing can never be perfect. That is because of the very of language. There are two sides to linguistic communication – the communicator and the receiver. Only when a reporter makes sense to the largest section of readers does he or she qualify to be a professional writer. The first draft of any writer may need a lot of tightening up, chipping and polishing. So the reporter should rewrite whenever his first effort is unsatisfactory for the reader's sake.

Even, so a reporter hard-pressed to meet deadlines may be left with hardly any time to rewrite his or her copy. So, when he sits down to write, be disciplined and alert in the structuring and construction of his reports. Place the important points at the precise junctures of his story. Invariably one needs to revise the copy and make it crisp.

Q18. Define Sports Reporting. Discuss the structure of Sports Reporting.

Ans. Sports journalism focuses on reporting amateur and professional sporting news and events. Sports journalists work in all media, including print, television broadcasting and the Internet. It is news writing. It has the structure of an action story but with greater freedom of style in writing. It is considered a specialised field; therefore, the sports writer is expected to possess certain qualities not so common among beat reporters. Aside from having a "nose for news," he should also:

- Have interest in all sports events
- Know the rules and regulations of the event or game he is writing about, and
- Have a working knowledge of the language and jargon of sports writing usually referred to as sports lingo.

The art of successful sports reporting and writing, is the art of fully knowing the various popular games and sports. The sports reporter must endeavour to write a news item or feature on any game/sport with the objectives of making it appealing to a particular class of readers interested and involved in those games/sports, and to captivate the minds of even those who are not exactly keen or fond of sports. Even as all sports games are competitive, so too are the areas of sports writing and reporting. In such a scenario, as a sports reporter he needs to structure his story around the reader's interest. He is sure to win readers in larger numbers if he brings the sports page of the newspaper alive in his report of the action on the playing fields. He needs to be thorough with his facts and capable of churning out a report under pressure of meeting a deadline. This way he will have an edge over sports reporters.

The structure of sports reporting is as follows:

- **How to Begin:** A sports reporter should always carry a notebook and pen with him. There are many who suggest that a journalist should have paper and pen at hand even when sleeping. He may get an exclusive idea when in bed! Renowned sports journalists are known to have formed the habit of jotting down every idea or scrap of information that comes their way. It is also rewarding to prepare notes on the end-pages of the books he reads. It is essential for journalists to preserve the material that they have collected.
- **Clipping Collection:** A reporter should develop a habit collecting clippings, interesting articles and news reports from newspapers and magazines can be collected on daily basis. Clippings can be filed under the appropriate subject or head. Or the reporter can have an office file to segregate the news clippings in each important discipline. So, start the clipping collection right away. Separate files can be made for each game. The simplest way to file press-clippings is to use large, thick envelopes marked "cricket", "football", "hockey", "athletics", etc. Or, you can have an office file to segregate the news clippings in each important discipline. So, start the clipping collection right away. That will be like a ready-made library. Timeliness and accuracy are of paramount importance to sports reporting in daily newspapers. Information and some views of a handful of experts can be obtained from these clippings. Apart from, these clippings can be referred for facts and figures. Facts are keys to analysis and comment.

- **In Search of Ideas in Sports:** A sport reporter must develop his own powers of observation. He must always be on the look out for an idea and keep an eye open for any interesting; out of-the-ordinary themes. Anything can be developed into a thought or an idea for an article or a feature. Therefore, never consider any material too trivial for a news item. Simply probe it for its news-worthiness so as to reach them sports page of a newspaper. It is part of training to learn to look at life with a journalist's eye. He needs to be sensitive to sights and sounds. A good sports journalist has to be conversant with important person in sports but also has to be equally proficient with the technicalities of sports. Ideas come during the course of conversation. But looking for ideas will be more rewarding than waiting for them to come up. Reporters must mix with people and intermingle with them.
- **The Ignition Point in Idea-Finding:** The ignition point in idea-finding is neither automatic, nor does it come readily. The reporter should remain on alert all the times. He should be watchful, patient and gather as much experience as he can. Thereafter, he can be sure to locate and identify ideas. He must also believe that inspiration will come to those who can master their disinclination. The writer's best work is often done when, feeling off-colour, he has had to face himself to write something.
- **Putting Ideas in Writing:** A writer should think clearly before writing down his thought. If the writer himself is unsure of what he wants to say, he is bound to leave a poor impression on readers. If a reporter does not have the habit of clear, constructive thinking, his story will reflect the hotpotch of his thoughts. Clear thinking helps in write a thought-provoking piece in lucid style. Besides, it generates a flow in ideas. A reporter should compare his writing with others. Self-analysis is better way to improve one's writing.

Q19. What types of quality must required in a sport reporter?

Ans. In order to write well, reporter must develop an easy, conversational style and tone that enables him to gain and hold the attention of the readers. Reporter must learn to write simple sentences and use simple words instead of resorting to high-sounding words. Sport report should be written in a simple style. Cliches, jargon and slang words should be avoided. Hackneyed expressions have no place in good reports. Such phrases as 'it may be recalled', 'it goes without saying', 'last but not the least', etc., reduce the impact of the news item or story.

A. P. Saxena (Pilloo), one of the most respected and successful news editors of the Indian Express, New Delhi, used to advise talented sports reporters to learn to use words that interest people. "It is not wrong to use words which draw the attention of the readers", said Pilloo once, adding: "Words familiar in tennis to table tennis may be used in cricket, if you know the art of using them."

- **Importance of a Fresh or New Angle:** Every sports reporter is faced with the task of discovering a fresh angle to a sporting event. A Reporter would probably be up against this kind of difficulty in the beginning of his career as a sports journalist. Think, and think deeply and calmly as to which particular wicket, partnership or catch in a cricket match, or a goal in a hockey or a football match, or gain of crucial point in a game of badminton, table tennis, saw the event changing course. In short, contemplate on the turning point. Reporter must highlight these turning point to prove his point of view. If he takes the right and professional approach, he will find that the readers will read his entire report through.
- **Reporter Must Keep Eyes and Ears Open:** Even if a sport reporter has good writing abilities and good network of contacts, he must do research before writing a report. He should keep his ears and eyes on the alert. Sometimes, even an innocuous meeting or drab cocktail party may provide a clue, or a lead for a sensational exclusive story, known as a 'scoope' in the newspaper world. Even if it looks like a gossip or a rumour, the reporter must get it confirmed from its sources. If it is confirmed that such thing has happened that can be a scoop for the news publication the reporter is working.
- **The Professional Approach:** A good reporter piece or report must be thorough in all aspect of the match. He must write for the people who were not lucky enough to be present at the site of the match. If his reader happens to have followed the score

or watched the match on the electronic media, then his report will be read for the analysis, expression and the points he highlight. When he writes a sports report, he must first consider which point he would like to highlight in his lead. Reporters report will be original only when he lends a fresh perspective on the sporting event. The must give his best to the report that he has written. If a reporter has this kind of attitude, he will find success and gain readership.

- **Writing to Length:** Precise-writing is the most important aspect of sports journalism. The more precise reporter is the more he will impress his readers. It being the jet age, readers are generally very busy. They do not have the time to read lengthy and vague news items, and instead are attracted toward crisp copy.

The report should have just the right amount of information so that it reads well and at the same time he meets the approved length. This is an integral part of the technique of professional sports journalism. It would help if he could be informed about the extent of space allotted to his news story. Accordingly, he could fit in his ideas. It is better for him to revise his own copy thoroughly before he submits it at the sports desk. This way could turn in a report that is near-perfect.

Q20. How does a reporter report and write the sports news?

Ans. When a reporter report sports events and issues, he must know how to find the news and write the report. Most importantly, he must get along with people of varying natures. He must also know the politics of his news medium. The most important thing is that a reporter wanting to make mark in the profession must inspire confidence. He should, therefore, know landmarks in the history of the game, its rules, terms and top ranking players of the sport he cover. The background information and achievements of players should be on his finger tips. In addition, he must the coaches, mangers, officials and office-bearers of various prominent clubs and associations. They he will be able to secure or extract some information from them when he needs to substantiate his report.

Sports news includes college sports at the amateur level and professional sports. The latter category includes regional national and international sports in the form of meets/matches. For instance, a meet in athletics, swimming, gymnastics, weightlifting or wrestling. Good sports writing is good news writing. Sports news reporting is slightly different from general reporting because a sports reporter enjoys greater freedom of self-expression. Such freedom includes the use of superlatives. Even among sports reporters, this freedom is generally given to those who are experienced and knowledgeable. All the same, one should rely on accurate and objective writing, stressing simplicity and clarity while avoiding unfamiliar terminology.

Reporters should also avoid writing vague reports. They are useless and leave no impression on the readers. Reports must provide details on the fitness of players, points of play, individual performance, tactics and strategies adopted in the contest and crowd reaction. To be a successful, sports reporter one has to cultivate one's power of observation and describe vividly what one sees. Writers must choose their words with care when writing about stars and professional players. Reporters must have documentary evidence before they comment about players (mis) deeds on and off the ground. The profession is quite hazardous and reporters must play safe while writing about some players, coaches or sports bodies:

(1) Need for Specialization: The arena of sporting activities is needed a vast one. A sports reporter has to know something about every sport: at least the salient features, norms, rules and regulations. Further, he has to specialise in one or two disciplines, say a combination of any turn of the following areas: cricket, hockey, football, tennis, badminton, table tennis, athletics, diving, gymnastics or swimming. Please note that this list is not exhaustive. Much depends upon reporter is interest and inclination. A sports reporter deficient in qualifications and ability may outplay a rival by sheer knowledge and dedication.

Specialisation, however, comes much later in one's career graph. Initially, the cub reporter must build a reputation of being capable of meeting regular changes in editorial needs. Therefore, reporter must train himself to write on a variety of topics. At the same time, he must also specialise in style that is both refreshingly different and illuminating to the general reader. To succeed in this, all that is required is accuracy of reportage and an original style of writing.

(2) Facts for the Advance Story or News Item: An assortment of facts may be available from reporter own library of news clippings; still, he has to depend upon the concerned officials, coaches and managers to get details for an advance copy. The better relations with officials, the more information will get from them. In the face of a defeat, an officials may yet be willing to speak to provided the two of enjoy a good equation. In a winning moment, doubtless anyone who is someone, would like to be quoted! Sport, particularly international sport, is no longer a matter of coordination of limbs. It is essentially being played at the metal level. The temperament and psychology of the players are equally, if not more important than technique and skill. Some teams or individuals succumb under pressure, while some rise to the occasion in the face of intense competition. This is the most vital aspect of sports and reporter has study it before penning down the reason for a loss or win. Further, sports reporters must exercise tact and perhaps persistence when seeking information from officials. They need to study the situation well before asking questions for example to the coach or the manager. Whatever information the reporter gather in this way will provide him with content enough for him advance report.

(3) Covering the Game: A sport reporter must learn to take notes systematically. He must remember all the important incidents and happenings including the major moves or strategies that had a bearing on the outcome. Watch the match dispassionately and without getting unduly excited.

When reporter writes his copy, he must remember the story. This is the first rule in sports writing. Avoid showing off his vocabulary, style or terminology. Do not inject colour and drama unless the situation demands such a report. If the match is dull and drab, he says so. Report the action of the sport or game in as much detail as the word limit permits. There is no strict rule or formula for a sport reporter; there are some conventional rules about the structure of the sports story. These are listed below:

(i) The Lead: Like any other news story, a sports story has a lead and a body. The sports lead is the attention-getter, the news in a-nut-shell. The classic five W's appear in the sports lead as:

(a) Who won?

(b) Against whom?

(c) By what score?

(d) Where? and

(e) When?

(ii) Major details: star players, breaks and weather, if necessary.

(iii) **Minor details:** other players, other plays and the behaviour/description of spectators.

(iv) **Other details:** statistics, line-ups and substitutions.

The summary lead should include the score and important details or the highlights, for example, the injuries, or the strategies, or the turning point of the match. In sport reporting, hard facts are more important than rich language and colourful expression. A report with facts can score over other reports. Simple language and original expression are suitable for sports writings.

The follow-up story is usually written at leisure, incorporating analysis and comment. In the follow-up story, information will be updated. There are also instances when the first report itself includes analysis. A reporter has to write under the pressure of deadline.

Q21. Write short notes on the followings:

(i) Sports Features and Columns

Ans. Apart from day to day reporting you may be called upon to write human interest stories, features and columns once you gain more experience and competence. It is said that "society is founded on hero-worship." Glorification and adulation of sports heroes – amateur and professional – occurs because of the increase in public interest and public following. But while writing sport features and column, the reporter should exercise moderation in praise and also in criticism. He must display responsibility in all his writings and he must bear in mind the laws of the press. His 100 brilliant pieces will be nullified with one lost court case. Exercise care and a balanced attitude in his writings, particularly when he is highlighting the negative trait of the personality of a player, or an important office-bearer of a sports body, national or international.

(ii) Sub-Editing Copy for the Sports Page

Ans. In some newspapers in India, a sports reporter is also required to work at the sports desk. This work involves subbing (or sub-editing) of the copy in addition to reporting on the 'beat'. Of sub-editors, it is said: "It's just a matter of fitting words of facts. The snugger the fit, the better the story. An efficient and competent sub-editor dresses up facts, marshals them and lets them march."

While every reporter has to develop a flair for writing, the 'sub' has to undergo training in the varied areas of editing, giving headlines and keeping them within certain space allocations, so as to prevent overset. Except for one or two newspapers in the country, all other papers have their own sports department which, apart from being autonomous, handles reporting, subbing and page-making. Generally, it is five or seven member sports journalists team that reports the games, edits the stories, and makes the pages.

(iii) Sports Page Make-up

Ans. The principles of page making are the same, be if for the sports page or any other page. On the strength of the significance of the news, a sub-editor draws up the dummy, makes enough provision for photographs so that the page comes alive with action-filled pictures instead of looking dull and drab. A good and lively photograph makes the page throb with life.

Q22. List the various tips which will help the sub sports reporter.

Ans. Following tips will surely help the cub sports reporter:

- Study the rules of the game in question.
- Study their history.
- Be on the mailing lists of bodies that govern sports.
- Cultivate friendly relations with officials of various clubs and associations.
- If any reporter with to specialise in reporting a particular sport, he must first acquaint himself with every aspect of the sport/game.
- At the beginning of every sporting season, interview well-known sports personalities in their respective field and enquire about their plan and programme for the forthcoming season.
- He read the journals pertaining to his particular sport.
- If reporter is not working on a computer, typewrite on one side of the sheet and use black ribbon.
- Double or triple space the lines so as to edit the copy easily.
- Leave enough space at the top, bottom and either sides of the page.
- Number and identify all sheets.
- Do not write more than one story on a page.
- Prepare copies in duplicate or triplicate.

- Write name in the upper left, corner below the slug.
- End each page on a paragraph. Write 'more' at the end of each page expect the last one.
- Try not to have confrontation with players and officials. He is paid to write, not to have arguments with stars and officials during or after the match.
- Players are an excitable lot. They are tolerable when they are successful, but they are difficult when they are passing through a lean patch. Leave from alone.
- The reporter does not strain his relations with a sub. One occasions, she/he may has destroyed copy but on many days she/he has rendered the copy readable and lively. S/he must develop a healthy relationship with him/her just as a player must respect the sentiments of the umpire.
- There is no sports reporter who does not err. Accept the laps instead of trying to defend the indefensible.
- Do not view things with a jaundiced eye. Have a positive outlook and think constructive.

Q23. Describe the meaning and concept of Development Reporting.

Ans. The concept of development journalism is not new, although the term itself came into common journalistic usage only during the early sixties. Like so many labels, its definitions can be stretched to embrace a number of subjects and issues. Development journalism could be dull and boring. However, well done, it is readable and informative. It could also be educative and inspirational, particularly the innovative experiments and success stories being undertaken to improve the human conditions throughout the country particularly in small towns and villages.

Development Reporting can be Defined as: "Development journalism seeks to report a country's progress and setbacks in both urban and rural areas in a factual and readable way. It should create an information bridge between the authorities and the public, between urban and rural communities. Long term, it aims to contribute to improvements in people's lifestyles."

Development reporting stands for removal of poverty, lessening of poverty between regions, classes and different sections of society, building up to technological infrastructure and modernisation of society through education. It is measured in terms of the improvement in the lives of the people.

Development reporting is somewhat different from routine reporting from court, legislatures, crime, science and technology or sports.

Ever since India adopted a process of planned development through the five year plans in 1951, rapid transformation have taken place in all walks of life in the country. Some of these changes have been welcomed by the people, but many developments have been opposed by them. Moreover, as development takes place, numerous new issues are thrown up which become controversial and assume the shapes of agitation, protests and dharnas. As a developmental reporter, he will be required to help in creating awareness about these developmental issues. The main task will involve informing readers, listeners, and viewers about the various plans, programmes, schemes and projects drawn up by government and different government agencies. A move widely accepted definition among the communication, states that the "development is a processes which facilities and results in participation and advancements, both material and social, of the widest possible number of people in a given society.

Development reporting needs some special skills, preparations, and qualities to be imbibed by reporters of print or electronic media. To be able do this job successfully, a reporter has to collect information on different development programmes.

(1) Styles of Development Reporting: Development has also negative effects like widespread pollution of air, water and soil, besides deforestation. This compels people and policy-makers to rethinking on what constitutes development and has given rise to several questions which development reporters have to write about. Development is required to provide not only food hygiene and health, nutrition and security but also ecological protection. It has enhanced the responsibility of the reporters. A reporter thus has to arrange his report logically.

(i) He has to collect data on the area which is being developed. This may involve interviewing the people for whom the development projects have been planned and also the authorities concerned with planning, implementation, and monitoring.

(ii) In writing development stories, the reporter has to be equipped with factual information which is generally not easily available.

(iii) He will has to develop his own outlook which is more important than styles and techniques.

(iv) The language of the reporter must be as simple as possible. When he mentions the figure of development, expenditure, population, income, etc. round up these instead of using fractions. The expression "Your income will be doubled if you take a crop of mungbeans during summer", is more effective than to give the exact figure of incomes raised in experimental plots in different areas.

(v) Comparative figures always help. For example, when the reporters on the impact on any new technology, dig up information before the introduction of technology and compare it with the change brought about after the adoption of new technology.

(2) The Development Process: The Process of development is generally slow, because people are slow in adopting novel ideas. For example, though extensive researches have established the potentials of growing high yielding varieties of grains, the process of adoption of the varieties is slow. Many people are displaced when their lands are acquired, to build roads, dams, and power stations etc. The process of development also requires people's participation and acceptance. It is here that the development reporter explains to the people the rationale behind building roads, schools and hospitals, use of high yielding resistant varieties, on the use of organic fertilizers and other such matters.

Although the government has spent billions of rupees on different development programmes in the seven five year plan since 1951, not much has been achieved in terms of making masses literate, providing them the basic minimum needs, increasing the per cent capita income and generally uplifting their living standards. On the other hand, a lot of damage has been done in the name of development. For example, the Food and Agricultural Organisation (FAO) estimates that over 75 percent of the annual global deforestation of 17 million hectares occurs for expanding food production. Irrigation without proper drainage results in soils getting alkaline or saline. Indiscriminate use of pesticides, fungicides and herbicides causes adverse changes in biological balance as well as leads to an increase in the incidence of cancer and other disease. Massive industrialisation without checks on releasing effluents and smoke results in dangerous levels of toxic chemicals in air, water and soils. Therefore, the process of development has become very complex and in many parts of the world the people are opposing large development programmes, almost to the extent of attaining an anti-development attitude. All these issues need to be presented to the people and the authorities. Development reporters in all mass media can help a great deal in this direction.

Q24. Identify the areas of Development Reporting.

Ans. There are many government and voluntary bodies, large institutional sector, or research institutions and several noted researchers and scientists doing a lot of good work for the country. If a reporter tries to find out development stories, there are thousands of them lying buried under reams of paper and stored in labs which never see the light of day.

There are many development news and ideas which are only casually or rarely covered in the media. A dedicated reporter can get many breaking development stories if he attempts to get and report them.

Many state and central government departments and ministries issue handouts, press releases, news letters, annual reports and a plethora of other publications, a reporter can get ideas from them as well. These materials can also be used for future references. When the reporter gets an idea talk to the concerned scientists or administrators and he can report a wonderful story. He can also meet people involved in researches in labs and libraries. A reporter can also get ideas at seminars, symposia and conferences. The news books and research journals are myriad provide new idea for development reporting. A reporter needs to keep up with the latest trends in the world of science and human endeavour.

(1) Tasks of Development Reporting: A development reporter has three tasks to perform – inform, interpret, and promote. If properly executed, a development reporter's job is more exacting than that of mere news reporters. A development report must be included with a noble motive of supporting, crusading or promoting a cause. A sincere development writer's role in the overall progress of the country is as vital as that of a person working with his own hands. Indeed, there are many attractions to trap a development reporter. Five star cocktails and dinner parties, foreign trips, precious gifts and simply bribing. A development journalist must develop a sixth sense to smell the rot before it envelops him. Avoid "mouthpiece writing" at any cost. But this is a very difficult task, bedecked with unlimited hurdles. Reporting failure is bound to annoy a lot of people. But that is the first and foremost task of a development reporter. Besides, the reporter must be honest to highlight the achievements and laurels won by the people executing the schemes.

(i) **Fostering a wide range of contacts:** A development reporter must nature contacts at the national level with development departments, ministries or rural development, agriculture, environment and planning, social welfare, child and women development, scientific institutions and universities.

He should also develop contacts in the information departments of states and public or private sector institutions. These are the sources where a reporter can get ideas for development stories.

(ii) **Contacts with international organizations:** A reporter must develop contacts with international organization like The United Nations, United Nations Development Programme (UNDP). Food and Agriculture Organization (FAO), World Food Programme, UNICEF. World Health Organisation (WHO), International Labour Organization (ILO), UNIDO (United Nations Industrial Development Organization). The United Nations is the biggest organization responsible to help the countries in development. These organizations frequently publish reports on their area of activity at the global level. A reporter must develop contacts with public information officers of these organizations.

(iii) **Keep a desk diary:** There are occasions when the reporters can get specific materials from different sources. For example, on occasions like World Health Day (April) and World Food Day (October 16), seminars and symposia are conducted. A desk diary will remind him about all these happenings and keep a track of them.

(iv) **Maintain your own reference material:** Reporters should also keep a record of published development features, articles, general stories, pamphlets, leaflets, reports and any printed document of relevance. These materials become reference for future writings. However, these day internet has become a very useful tool for reporters to get a reference just by click. Reporters can get various websites of organisations and government where they can get references easily.

(2) Specialised Skills Required for Development Reporting: Development reporting encompasses a number of areas. Every field needs and demands special skills to report on that particular area fully and competently.

Over 70 percent of India's population subsists on agriculture directly or indirectly. Therefore, agricultural progress and development in the rural areas are the most important areas of development reporting. Scientific research has undoubtedly transformed the countryside in all aspects by transferring technologies from labs to land.

To report on these developments, a reporter needs to collect information and present them in a right format with appropriate style and technique. He must avoid technical jargon and present them in a simple language. A reporter must tap every source of information. There are about 250 periodicals on farming, which provide basic information on agriculture and useful data on rural development. Besides, there are various government programmes which are being implemented such as the Integrated Rural Development Programme (IRDP), National Rural Employment Programme (NREP), Training of Rural Youth for Self Employment (TRYSEM), Development of Women and Children in Rural Areas (DWCEA) and Rural Landless Employment Guarantee Programme (RLEGP). All these programmes need impartial and objective scrutiny at every stage of their execution. There are weaknesses and shortcomings in their implementation. Efforts are there, but there are still an estimated 200 million people living below the poverty line mostly in rural areas.

A reporter can choose any programme and monitor its progress. Reporters can help in finding our why the target people are getting the benefits of these schemes. Journalists can also help in mobilizing people's participation in these projects. There are also many other areas for developmental reporting such as health and hygiene, social and economic issues, women and children's welfare, industrial development, energy and environment, literacy and adult education, population and family planning, marriages and other customs. Besides, a reporter should look for new issues which come up everyday.

Q25. How a development reporter should adopt the media and adapt his/her skills to suit the characteristics of various media?

Ans. A development reporter has to take different approaches to present his report. We discuss how a reporter should adopt the media and adapt his skills to suit the features of various media.

Development Reporting for Press: In development, reporting the press is seen as a mechanism of communal impartiality and a tool for achieving beneficial social change. In other words, the media should carry out positive development tasks in line with nationally established policy.

As a development reporter, he will be required to process and present facts in an intelligible form to the reader/viewer/listener. Although electronic media, radio and television, have made a veritable impact on the masses, print media will remain most decisive and educative for a long time to come. In India, print medium occupies an important place. There are more than 1500 daily newspapers published in all the 18 national and other languages. Several newspapers devote full pages to development news. For example, The Indian Express, The Pioneer, and The Hindu in English set aside one full page for "Development News" once a week. Development stories are best done in the form of a feature article. Newly started development work or those proceeding at a snail's space, thereby leading to tremendous loss in funds causing terrible inconvenience to the public can be presented in the form of news items or featurised news stories.

In fact, photo feature on development projects can also be presented effectively. Interviews with the recipients of the benefits of the projects already completed can also help evaluate their impact on the masses. Such writings can also induce authorities to expedite other projects under implementation.

An Imaginative development writer can do free lancing for the press, radio, and television. Besides employment, opportunities exist in different newspaper establishments to cover development news. A development reporter however has a challenging job and requires hard work, commitment and dedication. But the compensation in terms of contribution to the national development are tremendously satisfying.

Development Reporting for Radio: In India, radio has proved its utility as a potent audio medium for creating awareness among people in several areas of human endeavour, including development. It helps in promoting an instinctive urge for development consciously, by broadcasting programmes designed to help people diagnose their problems and clarify their objectives so that they may be able to make their decisions more wisely. India has of late witnessed tremendous expansion in the two electronic media, radio and television. From six radio stations in 1947, All India Radio (AIR) has grown to nearly 200 radio stations, catering to the local and regional audiences. Rural Radio Forums were started in 149 stations. Seven radio stations were used for broadcasting 20 programmes to 150 village groups clustered in five unilingual districts of one state in the first pilot project. Each forum consisted of 10 to 20 villages. They gathered to hear and discuss programmes. An elected secretary kept minutes of the meetings, while a chairperson (who was elected for short term) led discussions.

The forums often raised questions about new problems and appealed to AIR for additional information or for advice on how adapt information to the local conditions. A typical programme devoted 20 minutes to a substantive agricultural issue and ended with a 10 minutes dialogue in response to questions raised by previous programmes. Brief comments on market reports and weather were also aired. Listeners and participants in forum groups could hear as many 50 hours of radio programming. They could also experience as many as 100 opportunities to participate in, or hear subsequent local discussions. Evidence from carefully conducted field experiments confirmed that the Indian government's "grow more food" campaign had been stimulated by this combination of mass media, interpersonal communication and subsequent feedback. Field experiments which compared villages with "rural radio forums to villages without them were filled with praise." ... a success beyond expectations.

Increase in knowledge in the forum villages was spectacular, whereas in the non forum villages it was negligible. Growth of the relatively cheap transistor radio, reduced the villagers' desire to attend forum meetings. They preferred to stay home and listen to other types of programmes. This led to their demise, although some listeners' clubs are still operating.

Regular radio farm and home units have been established in all the radio stations headed by farm radio officers to run agricultural and rural development programmes. About 20 radio stations have science cells headed by "science officers." Various campaigns against smoking and drugs were carried through radio with the help of experts.

Thus, as a development reporter for radio, there is plenty of scope to write scripts, to devise special programmes and also the work in the capacity as a free lancer to do development field stories.

Development Reporting for Television: As a development reporter, you can use television to spread know-how, to as many people as within the reach of a television centre or even to the whole country through national hook-up. However, to be effective, your development programme must be field-based. You must remember that television is a visual medium. And if visuals are missing or the cameraman fails to focus on the relevant visuals, then the television's impact will be completely lost.

For making a good television programme with a view to motivate people for development requires a lot of effort, research, and commitment. In 1975, some researchers undertook the task of developing audience profiles of the people who were likely to receive television programmes through SITE - Satellite Instructional Television Experiment transmission. Each profile contained information on a cluster of three to four districts in a sate, covering aspects such as language, customs, values, beliefs, social structure, economy, agriculture, health, hygiene, nutrition, mother-child care and family planning. Television programmes could be telecast to support development programmes in all these spheres.

For writing a good television script, fewer words and more visuals are needed. Much more is communicated through visuals. You may first shoot the film according to a rough script, or you may first write the complete script and then take up shooting according to it. It works both ways. It is better to involve yourself at every level of the production of such a programme. If you just write the script and give it to a producer and do not accompany the camera team for shooting at the site, the programme may miss some of the vital points.

Reporting on Sustainable Development: The term "sustainable development" was popularised by the report of the World Commission Environment and Development (WCED), also called the Bruntland Report with the title "Our Common Future" published in 1987. A strategy for sustainable living tiled "Caring for the Earth" prepared by the International Union for Conservation (IUCN), the UNEP (United Nations Environment Programme) and the World Wide life fund (WWF) defines sustainable development as "improving the quality of human life while living within the carrying capacity of supporting ecosystem." According to Dr. M.S. Swaminathan "A dynamic concept of carrying capacity would imply in operational terms the conservation of natural ecosystems as well as their continuous improvement through research, training, technology, community cooperation and public policies.

To some, sustainable development is a long waited call for political recognition of global environmental decay, economic injustice and limits to material growth. Economics driven growth has led to a 20-trillion global economy. The decline in environmental quality has however underlined the need for harmonizing the logic of economics with that of ecology. A destructive consequence of human action is the gradual conversion of the surface of the earth into wastelands and degraded lands. Globally, 15 percent of the total earth surface has undergone human induced soil degradation. About 24 percent of the human-occupied territory of the earth is degraded only by human activities. At least 66 million hectares of irrigated land is affected by Stalinization. About 1 million hectares of it prime farmland in rain fed areas is being lost each year to urbanization. There are also similar frightening figures with reference to water pollution and ground water exhaustion. Compounding these problems is the gradual diversion of forest lands for a variety of other uses, thereby resulting in the loss of habitats rich in biological diversity.

According to Dr. M.S. Swaminathan ("From Stockholm to Rio-de Janerio: The Road to Sustainable Agricultural" 1987), the problem facing us today is not so much of discovering what must be done to ensure sustainability, as learning how to do it. The technologies which can promote sustainability rely heavily on knowledge as a substitute for capital, farm grown inputs as substitutes for market purchased ones and community co-operation as a supplement to individual action.

3 WRITING FOR THE PRESS

INTRODUCTION

Good writing is all about choosing the right words to say precisely what we mean. Good writing is not a luxury; it is an obligation. It is something long, wonky and barely understandable to the average human being. "Good writing" is only something that the elite can possibly accomplish. There is hardly a person who does not read. A good book write-up remains so whatever language it may be written in. There are various techniques for feature writing in news. Until independence in 1947, Indian newspapers, being preoccupied with political affairs with particular emphasis on the struggle for freedom, devoted little space to features. Even today, political coverage remains their staple diet, with a curious obsession with speeches of political leaders not only in the central and state legislature but also at public functions, rallies and press conferences. Opinion and editorial writing are also important for writing for the press. The opinion is a piece of writing that expresses the personal belief of the writer about timely issues. It is supported by facts. It regularly appears each issue under the same title and at the same location on the page. An editorial is an expression of facts and opinions in concise or an analytical interpretation of significant and timely topics or issues. It is logical and pleasing in order to influence opinion, or to interpret significant news such that its importance to the reader will be clear.

Q1. Describe in detail the various characteristics of good news writing and qualities of good writing as well.

Or

What are the habits that acquire to be a Good Writer?

Ans. Eminent journalist M.V. Kamath says, "A good write-up is a study in effortlessness. It must flow freely. It must be knowledgeable without being pretentious, entertaining without being vulgar and informative without being newsy". This sums up what a good write-up is, be it an article, essay, reportage or whatever form of writing it may be. Kamath says, the essence of his career spent in the profession of writing. But who aspire to be writers and achieve great heights, certainly cannot get to it unless they practice writing, or get to know the basics of what this art is.

To be a good writer, a reporter must be a good reader as well. Question may be raised on what to read and what not to read. A novice writer should start reading everything. He must read good books, newspapers, magazines and journals. Visit any library. Browse through the catalogue and check the books in the shelves. Initially, start with some classics. Shakespeare still is fresh and robust. His style remains inimitable. A reporter should read him and at the end, he will find that there has been a sea change in his approach and imagination. If he does not want to read Shakespeare then start with any book. When he begins, the book may not be worth reading, but once he starts and get into the habit, he would know gradually what more to read. Never be fobbed by the high-sounding names of writers. Do not get into the inferiority complex syndrome. Just knowing the names of big writers alone, does not take us where we want to reach.

The aim should be learning and for that a reporter can start virtually anywhere. It can be a nice fairy tale like the Aesop's Fables or the abridged version of Jonathan Swift's Gulliver's Travels or simply whatever he can lay his hands on. Howsoever bad, a writer has certainly gone through the deals which he is yet to set sail on. If he is a discerning reader, in fact, he will learn the crux of what bad writing is. Once he knows the bottom line, he will learn his first lesson – not to write in a bad manner. His curiosity to better his skills automatically comes to him.

This is true not only for English, but also if he wants to take up writing as a profession in any other language. Remember, the basics remain the same. The language may differ but the basic concepts never change. A good book or write-up remains so whatever language it may be written in. Else, why should people look for translations of Omar Khayyam or the Odyssey or the Mahabharata? As we read any of these classics, we are struck with the simple and attractive style. The very first lesson in good writing is that we have to write in a simple manner so as to make it acceptable to an editor of sub-editor, who is likely to patience, hard-work and an understanding of what our reader needs. Writing is not easy. Yet if we want to be a writer "all we do is sit down and just go on writing", that is what eminent writers say.

Qualities of Good Writing are as follows:

- Good writing, particularly for the mass media, is clear, concise, to-the-point. It transmits information, ideas and feelings to the reader clearly but without overstatement. It is writing that outlines pictures of ideas which the reader fills in with his/her own imagination.
- It uses the minimum number of words to make its point. It is precise. As well -written piece uses words for their exact meaning. It does not throw words around carelessly or without cause.
- Good writing is modest. It does not draw attention to itself. Good writing does not try to show off the intelligence, or lack of it, of the writer. It lets the content speak for itself and it allows readers to receive message directly. Remember, people who like to read enjoy the ideas and information they get from reading.

Q2. How news story forms the basis of all writing?

Ans. To write well, a writer should have a thorough knowledge and understanding of the news event. Besides, he must know the basic structure of the news story and tradition of news writing. The basic principles of news reporting can be applied to virtually any kind of writing.

All Students of mass media should learn the news writing format if he has any plan to work for a newspaper. We are stressing on this as we believe that mastering the news story is the step on the road to mastering the mass media. People read newspapers or watch to news bulletin for "information". A news man looks for information wherever he goes or talks to people.

Thus, to be a good writer, particularly for the mass media, he needs to have two important tools. First, gathering information and second, transforming this information in an appropriate form.

Once a person knows this, he fulfils the basic requirement to becoming a writer. A news story requires simple, straight forward prose, clear thinking and a complete understanding of the subject on the part of the writer as well as conciseness and precision in the use of the language. All forms of writing for the mass media requires adherence to this rule.

Criteria of News Story: Some of the criteria that editors insist upon for selecting a story are: impact, timeliness, prominence, proximity, conflict, bizarre or unusual and currency.

- Impact is the effects or results of a story on the people. A policy decision by the Central government will have impact on the people of the whole country and all national and regional newspapers will carry the news. On the other hand, a policy by the Orissa government will not be carried by a regional newspaper in Kerala as it does not have any impact on the people of Kerala.
- Timeliness is also a key factor for any event. If the reporter had some material about arms dropping in some other land and could relate it to the arms dropping Purulia, it would have been a worthwhile exercise after the incident was reported.
- Prominence of people, place or incidents is a key factor in a news report. If a prominent people in involved, even trivial incident are read with great interest. For example, if Sachin Tendulkar in involved in a minor accident that will a front page story of all newspapers.
- Proximity is the distance and the area where the incident has happened. An event at home, your town, state or nation is more important than a happening 1,000 kilometres away. For example, five persons die in a road accident in Pune will get front-page coverage in Pune's newspaper, but it may not be carried by newspapers in Kolkata.
- Conflict always makes news. Conflict between two countries, two parties in an election or two groups becomes news. If there

is a fighting between two groups of traders or any other influential people in any locality, it can be a big news for any local paper.

- Bizarre or unusual incidents make news. Such events attract readers' attention. If a dog bites a man, it is not news, but if a man bites a dog, it is news.
- Currency is like timeliness, Issues that have the value of currency come and go, but there are always several such issues being discussed by the people. The food shortage in late 1960s is such an issue. The green revolution and family planning programmes during emergency in early 1970s and failing ecology in 1980s and the hawala in 1990s are also such issues. All newspapers carry these

How to Structure a News Story?: A writer should know how to build a story so that the most important and interesting information is presented to the reader in the most efficient manner.

In a news story the 5 Ws and 1 H– Who, What, When, Where, Why and How are very important. "Who" is the people related to the story. "What" is the major action of the story. "When" is time when the event takes place. "Where" is the location of the incident. "Why" and "How" are the explanations about events. They must come ahead of all other information in a news story.

Q3. Discuss how a reporter allows the readers to get as much information as possible through the Inverted Pyramid.

Ans. The news story is written in the inverted pyramid style with the most significant fact at the top. The other facts follow in their order of importance except in special circumstances. This enables a story to remain self-contained, no matter how much of it is deleted from the end. For this reason, the first "take" (part) of a news report must bring out the dramatic importance of the event.

Schools of journalism talk about a news story being composed like an inverted pyramid. This means that if we turn the pyramid on its head we have that broad base at the top. The board base of a well-written story is at the top, the intro and then the rest of the story following in a mixture of chronological order and importance so that the last sentences or paragraphs of the story are the least important.

There are two advantages in presenting the story in this inverted pyramid style. First, if the reader does not read to the end, that a number of readers do not, then they have still got the essential facts. And from production point of view, it is so much easier for the sub-editor, who will have to prepare the story to specific instructions of length, to be able to chop an inch or two right off the bottom of the story if he has to, rather than remove a word here and a sentence there.

The inverted pyramid style has developed in journalism over the years. In stories written in the above style, the climax is at the beginning in the lead. The reporter gives main information, then the secondary information. It is the traditional story structure.

Inverted Pyramid Format Assists: The reporter, who uses it to compose facts quickly, the editor, who can delete the last few paragraphs of a story to make it fit the page, and The reader, who can tell at a glance if he is interested in the story.

The format has been criticized as being old fashioned and traditional. However, the inverted pyramid has survived and will probably do so in future as well.

Q4. What is feature and magazine writing? Describe the essential components of feature writing.

Ans. A feature has a special style of writing and demands description in details. There can be no change in the facts related to news, but feature written on one subject in different papers has different style of description. A feature encompasses past, present and future. It does not only include the facts, but it is also built on the presumptions. For example, a writer of a feature covering the participating teams in the world cup (football) can make comments on the anticipated outcome of the event, wins & defeats, performance of the teams, ups & downs, etc. Making use of statistics, photos, colour transparencies, cartoons, charts & maps, etc. make a feature more interesting and eye-catching.

The process of writing a feature article is not much different from writing an article for a newspaper or newsletter. One of the main differences however, is that a feature article is designed to be written in a way that the information is not time-based, but is timeless. The key to writing a good feature article is to select the proper venue for the article and then to write the article directed at that audience.

A reporter should keep in mind the following points to write a good magazine article:

- A subject of compelling interest to the magazine's readers should be selected. Selection of interesting topics will not be difficult if a reporter knows the target readers.
- Spice the article with colourful or entertaining material examples, anecdotes and facts.
- To make the reader involved with the article or feature, establish a strong reader identity
- Writing should be clear, absorbing and to the point.
- The article should be appealing. Some subjects have more appeal than others.
- The rules that are good for news writing are also good for articles. They are proximity, prominence, timeliness, conflict, bizarre and currency.
- Other elements and glamour, sex, success, human interest and competition.

Q5. What are the techniques for Good Writing? Explain the suggestions for improving writing.

Ans. Writing is not simply an inherent talent that some of us may be having and some other won't be. There are steps that all of us can take, to improve our writing skills. Writing is a process. To produce a good write-up we have to learn to combine the rules, techniques and norms with own individual style. Writing is hard work, it is physically, mentally and emotionally demanding. Good writing does not happen all of a sudden. Writing can often be slow, tedious and even frustrating. Good writing does not happen all at once. It is the result of sweat and blood.

Given below are some of the suggestions that a writer can apply to produce a good write-up:

- **Write Simply:** The best way to achieve clarity in writing simple to convey their message. A novice writer will also find it easy to write in a simple manner.
- **Use Simple Words:** Big and complicated words do not impress the readers. In this regard, Benjamin Franklin once said, "To write clearly, not only the most expressive but the plaintest words should be chosen".

- **Use Simple Sentences:** Long winding sentences distract the readers. Readers read simple sentences with ease and enjoy reading.
- **Economise on Words:** Writers should use as minimum words as possible in their drafts. A careful Editor deletes unnecessary words while editing. There is no substitute for simple, straight and forward prose.
- **Do not use Jargon:** Writers should avoid use of technical words in their writings. Each subject has a technical language of their own, which is called jargon. They are understood only by the select group of people. As a writer, you should not use these. A write-up with cliches is not considered good writing.
- **Avoid Adjectives:** Writers should avoid use of adjectives and adverbs. Sentences should be built around nouns and verbs. Usage of adverbs and adjectives weaken message. A good verb denotes action and a better verb denotes action and description. Adverbs and adjectives modify and verbs expand your thoughts and thus the writing.
- **Tie Together- Avoid Jolts:** Writing must be well knit. All the facts and information presented in a story should be well linked to make a complete piece of write-up. Do not make the write-up disjointed.
- **Be Specific:** Readers avoid write-ups which have too many superfluous words and high-sounding words. To be specific, get to the point, sometimes, it is certainly a difficult task. But writers should focus on the points which they want to convey.
- **Avoid Repetition and Redundancies:** Sometimes facts get repeated in a write-up. Writers must avoid this It makes the copy disjointed and a bad write-up.
- **Cut Out Unnecessary Words:** Avoid words like 'really', 'actually', 'very' and 'in fact'. These words do not tell anything. Such words should be removed.

Q6. Discuss the need of Accuracy and Attribution in good writing.

Or

Discuss the role of accuracy and attribution in feature writing.

Or

Write a short note on Attribution.

Ans. Accuracy is very important in news writing. A journalist is aim should be achieve accuracy. To achieve the accuracy is not just a matter of the technique of writing but a state of mind that a reporter must foster. He should not be satisfied with false information, half-baked information or about something. He may have doubts about.

Make sure that dates and identifications are correct, numbers in a story add up properly and locations are correct. Do not consider that reader is a fool. He may not write a word in praise but he would not mind writing long letters to point out the silliest mistake may commit. If a reporter is not accurate, we will lose credibility – that is he will not enjoy the trust of the readers. Once he lose credibility as a writer he lose his market.

Spell Names Correctly: Reporters must write the correct spellings of names – the way the person concerned himself. There are also instances when a newspaper reports carry the multiple spellings of names. Reporters must double check the names at least.

Attribute Correctly: Misquoting or quoting out of context are very common. While at times, it is an alibi for a source to back out after the story has come out in print, in many cases the writers themselves are to be blamed. While talking to a source keep the cars open. Try to understand what he/she wants to say. In case of doubt, repeat the question. Do not think that the source would get annoyed. Even if he/she does, it is better to annoy one person than a host of readers and editors on whom the credibility rests.

Quotes can be direct and indirect. Effort should be to retain the words used by the source. However, if his/her grammar is faulty, it should corrected so that it is not ridiculed by others. Unless writing a satire or humorous piece, should not used wrong grammar. In an indirect quotation or paraphrase, there would be the liberty to express the views of the source in different words. The caution, however, is that it should not change the meaning.

Attribution is important. By revealing where a reporter has got his information from, he tells the reader whether it is reliable or not. In short, leave the assessment of the reliability of the information to the reader. This also saves him from the embarrassment of some information which may be misleading. Readers finally would blame the source – a department, ministry or official – and him for presenting incorrect information.

As attribution builds up credibility, although too much of it can get in the way of the story by affecting its flow, and too little of it can confuse the reader. A reporter has to maintain a balance between the two.

Q7. What are the sources and ideas of getting information about good writing?

Or

Write a short note on story idea.

Ans. A journalist is known as a person with ideas. A journalist is known as a person with ideas. A reporter always looks for new ideas. He needs to have new ideas and be able to evolve ideas into stories if he wants to be a good writer. Reporters sometimes "exclusive stories". These stories are called exclusive because the ideas and information are new or no newspaper have carried it.

To get news ideas, read between the lines. There may be many paragraphs, which may have some idea, which can be developed into an independent story. He needs to spend time to get ideas. He must meet people, call sources, visit places, laboratories and similar other places to get ideas.

A beginner has to develop news sense. He needs to go through newspapers to get story ideas. If there is news on the slump in rupee rates against dollar, he can develop that story in many ways. He can write on how other countries tackled such a situation. He can find whether it is an international conspiracy to weaken the Indian economy. If he is a magazine writer can develop this story a full cover stories with a research.

Magazines and sometimes house journals themselves are the sources of articles. Ideas do not have any copy right. Sometimes he can get ideas from the letters to the editor. He should have a clear idea of what he is writing about. He should have facts and references to support them.

A writer has three basic sources – people, records (stored information or files of a department or institution) and personal observation.

Most of the information he would get from personal sources. He also have to spend most of his non-writing time talking to people, either personally or on the phone. If is a beginner, develop friendship with a new person every day. Keep in touch with them he may not get a story the same day but he may get some brilliant ideas from them any time in future. Most of the people who have information will be interested to share it with him.

Top officials are always a better source. Even peons, receptionists and telephone operators can be a source his of articles. But to protect such sources, he must talk with the official concerned to confirm the news. They can be his regular sources.

Personal observation is another major source for reporters. He can find a story at any place may be while travelling, or while shopping in a market. His observation sometimes can bring out very offbeat copy, a humorous piece or an illuminating article.

Reporters can get good stories from stored sources. Such records can be found in scientific reports, government bulletins, trade journals, current books, speeches, museums, company records and papers of some famous persons and even old press releases. The records of a government department or even of some individual provide a big story idea. The Bofors scandal came out of such records – files. He can access most of the stored records through his personal contacts. Information from more than one of these sources can brighten his copy.

He must cross check information, give credit and attribution where it is due and tell the truth. The more information he build up the more it would help him and he will get new story ideas.

Q8. Write a short note on Revise and Rewrite.

Ans. Very few writers and those who have vast experience can express effectively without any mistake in a first draft. Writers should write down at the first flash of a thought in the best possible manner. The first thoughts are like building up a structure without the external and interior finishing's. Later on, he needs to polish his write-up. In second and third reading he will find out several errors or the story may not be structural properly. If he is a beginner, he should give his write-up to a friend to read. Ask him to look at the write-up in a critical angle.

Most writers write and then dump their writings on the editor's table. This is a wrong practice. Many silly mistakes may happen when they write. If they revise their copy they can correct them. Reporters must revise their copy after a few hours of writing. If time permits leave his write-up for a day or half a day, read it again and they will come up with certain discrepancies.

You will also feel to rewrite your copies during revision. During rewriting, you can add more information, delete superfluous items and go on changing or improving certain information. You should also keep in the basic criteria of a story.

While revising, they must check the spellings and the grammar. If he find any limitation in their copy or it has been difficult for them to understand, you can hold back their copy and get back to their source for additional information. Keep in view the deadline, may miss it while they are writing the copy or if they are holding the copy.

Q9. What is feature writing? Describe the essential components of feature writing.

Ans. A feature has a special style of writing and demands description in details. There can be no change in the facts related to news, but feature written on one subject in different papers has different style of description. A feature encompasses past, present and future. It not only includes the facts, but it is also built on the presumptions. For example, a writer of a feature covering the participating teams in the world cup (football) can make comments on the anticipated outcome of the event, wins & defeats, performance of the teams, ups & downs, etc. Making use of statistics, photos, colour transparencies, cartoons, charts & maps, etc. make a feature more interesting and eye-catching.

Features Compared with Other Forms of Writing: The technique of feature writing is similar to the technique of any expository, narrative or journalistic writing since it makes use of an introduction, a body, and a conclusion.

(1) The Feature Allows Latitude and Variety in Lead: Including, as it does, such a variety of expository, narrative or journalistic types, feature writing allows considerable latitude in striking the keynote of the article. Hence, the combination of any one of two or more of the following types:

- **(i) News Summary Lead:** Similar to that used in straight news writing, this lead is the condensed version of the whole story and embodies the 5W's and the H.
- **(ii) Distinctive-Incident Lead:** This snaps a word picture of the story in its most characteristic moment and at a point when it has reached its summit of dramatic interest.

(iii) **Quotation Lead:** A familiar quotation that is apropos to the theme of the story may be used to indicate to the reader what the story is going to be about.

(iv) **Short Sentence Lead:** This consists of a single striking assertion which may either be a summary of the whole story or a statement of the most significant facts.

(v) **Contrast Lead:** This is a statement of two obviously different facts with the purpose of emphasizing the fact that will be the theme of the article.

(vi) **Analogy Lead:** Similar to the contrast lead but it gains is effect showing the similarity between some well-known facts and the facts that will be the theme of the story.

(vii) **Picture Lead:** A graphic description o the setting of the story told in the article serves as an introduction to its action or the characters in it.

(viii) **Janus-Faced Lead:** A lead may look backward into the past or forward into the future for purposes of comparison with the situation in the present which is the theme of the story.

(ix) **Humorous Lead:** A humourous lend sets the tone of a feature perfectly for the reader. Example: Long experience has taught me that in Bombay nobody goes to the theatre unless he or she has bronchitis.

The Main Body is Developed as in Other Good Writing: Insofar as feature writing is similar to any other expository, narrative, or journalistic writing, the main body of the feature article is developed as in any other good writing. It should exemplify the three cardinal principles of unity, coherence, and emphasis in its separate paragraphs and in itself as a whole. This may be accomplished by (i) having a central theme or main idea carried throughout the article, (ii) eliminating extraneous material, and closely relating all the material in the article to the central theme,: and (iii) bridging the transition from each paragraph to the next one easily and smoothly avoiding abrupt changes of thought.

(2) The Conclusion is not Unlike that in Narrative Writing:

(i) It may be a condensed summary of the whole article, reviewing briefly the salient facts brought out in the article,

(ii) It may be a climax or the highest point of interest in the article, or

(iii) It may be a "cut-back" or "flash-back" to the introduction, i.e., a restatement of the lead phrased in a somewhat different language but serving to emphasize the important statements made at the beginning and to "round out" the whole article.

Q10. Describe the various types of features in feature writing.

Ans. A feature can be written on any subject. A reporter can write about a boy trying to cross a busy street, a cat wanting to catch an elusive rat, a nurse at work in a hospital, a vegetable vendor in street, men and women practising unusual professions, personal accounts of travel, reminiscence of the past – in fact, any subject can be turned into a feature. A feature has no specific length. It can be as short as four paragraphs or as long as 40 paragraphs. Features can be categorized as: news features, human-interest features, personality features, historical features, etc. Some of the features are discussed as follows:

(1) Human Interest Features: Human Interest features are now flattering more popularity in India. One can get ideas of such features in a number of ways. The major news headings of the day tell of the important happenings. The human-interest stories tell of how those happenings have impacted the people, animals, or places around the story. These are the stories that many of us read in detail. They are the ones that we bring-up in conversation with our friends. While we may scan quickly through the top news stories, we are intrigued by the details of how other people are dealing with these happenings. It makes events that may happen halfway around the globe seem more real to us. After all, people are people wherever they live. Reading about how they cope gives us some insight into how we might cope if we were in a similar situation. Human interest features may be written 'a day in the life of a common man', such as a constable, gardener, sweeper, beggar or a 102-year-old man', marrying the seventh time, or a sixty year old women giving birth to a child. The there is a story of a man who eats lizards, or glass.

The emphasis in these features is on the unique views of life or on unusual occupations. A feature writer may probe on subject such as 'gay' or lesbian' or heterosexuals'—why they behave as they do and from where they get the support. And many other human-interest stories are written to show a subject's oddity or its practical, emotional, or entertainment value. How to do, or utilize, or process features give direction and guidance on doing something, such as repairing or assembling of radio or television sets, childcare, making of dolls etc. such features should be on a definite and concrete piece of work. The directions should be simple, clear, and in logical sequence, so that they can be followed by readers without specialised knowledge or skill. Human-interest features deal with ordinary circumstances. They touch the heart of the reader and appeal to his emotions. It would be worthwhile to consider the following human-interest stories.

(2) Personal Narratives: Personality features are based on well-known persons and their achievements. In such features, the emphasis is on what has made the man great rather than cataloguing his achievements. A personality profile is written to bring an audience closer to a person in or out of the news. Interviews and observations, as well as creative writing, are used to paint a vivid picture of the person. Personality features may be written not only on newsworthy personalities or on great men who capture the imagination of people, but also on little known persons, such as a auto scooter driver who has become a multi millionaire. These features are not biographical sketches, features don't follow system or strategy and it is not necessary to tell the story from birth to death. Features have to be interesting and they shouldn't be bombarded with unwanted information. It is sufficient to give just enough background of the person and his recent achievements. A feature writer need not give all details or deal with all aspects. The objective is to tell the readers about the qualities of the man and how he has achieved the position of eminence. Many prominent writers have written about personality features in details hence it is not worth writing about the work, which is available to the learner hence its time to have an overview of the personality features.

(3) News Features: It appears in news columns but its news value content is lower as compared to hard news. Backgrounders, situationers and story describing 'how' of an even come in this category of features. Commonly these features are connected to current news, and one gets ideas of these features from the newspapers. A few instances are: Prime Minister's visit to the UK and US may give an idea about the motive behind the visit, the kind of people the Prime Minister would be meeting. This type of features revolve around the parameter of news and provides detailed report on the news which might have appeared in the newspapers or in other media a day or two earlier or might have appeared few months ago.

(4) Meeting Unusual People: The world is full of extraordinary persons whose life and work can make good features. An example was a feature on a German couple. Heribert and Maike Frank, whose chance encounter with a craftsman in Mysore led them to quit their plum jobs and create a 'little India' in their home town of Munchen.

(5) Travel Sketches: Travel fascinates most people even though they may be prevented by lack of money or time from visiting as many places as they may want to. Travel features satisfy a basic human desire to know more about the world we live in.

For Example: After a three-hour drive along winding mountain roads, with deep valleys on one side and huge menacing boulders jutting out of the rocks on the other, we arrived at snow-covered Nathu La to be greeted by the thin fleeting cloud of mist. The cloud passed by swiftly to reveal three Chinese climbing down the slope on the other side of the barbed wire-fence put up by our troops to demarcate the boundary.

(6) Historical Features: This type of features are written making various events the basis of the theme. Our daily life is a warp & woof of various events. These events, when have instantaneous or far-reaching consequences affective our lives, take the form of a feature.

For Example: Mysore lives in its fabled past. The history of the city takes off from a fort that Bettada Chamaraja Wodeyar, a feudatory of the Vijayanagara empire, build in 1584. He called the settlement 'Mahisura Nagar', which meant capital town. Another line of thought is that the city got its name from the legendary demon, Mahisha, vanquished by the goddess Chamundeswari, who now pre-sides over Mysore from the top of a hill.

(7) Interpretative Features: Interpretative features analyse facts and information. Such features are intended to inform and instruct the readers about the background and significance of various issues.

(8) Autobiographical Human Documents: Such features are written about the personal experiences or intimate personal matters.

"My Experiment with Truth' is a wonderful account of the personal experiences of Mahatma Gandhi.

(9) Science features: Features can be written on science and technology, scientific studies and innovation. Readers are interested to read about science and technology.

(10) Practical Guidance Features: Their features are intended to inform and guide the readers. Such features are designed to tell the reader how to make, repair or collect things.

(11) Miscellaneous: Features can also be written on various other subjects. We can write on mundane activities like gardening and cooking to unusual trades and professions, from fashions and good grooming to mountaineering and bird-watching. If we find news point on any topic, subject or issue that will be interesting, we can write.

Unusual Professions: Features can be written on unusual professions like puppeteers who have fallen on bad days, the leech doctor who may well claim to be a precursor of the modern surgeon, the street juggler and many others.

Q11. Write short notes on the followings:

(i) Quality People Read Edit Page

Ans. Newspapers are an important source of opinion making. This is done through every aspect of newspaper writing. Though newspapers have separate pages for news and views, opinions are at times interwoven with news items as explanations, backgrounds and interpretative paragraphs. This is so, particularly in respect of major developments and when the subject is not one with which the reader is expected to be familiar. Similarly, editorials or leader pieces contain essential background to support their arguments. A small section of readers turn to the edit page. These quality people are often better aware of important news than ordinary ones. Therefore, sometimes it is assumed that readers of editorial pages are generally aware of what has appeared in the news pages to appreciate the arguments and conclusions.

The "edit page" of a newspaper is essentially an opinion page. It is a prestigious part of the newspaper, which often gets the direct attention of the editor. It reflects the policy of the newspaper and makes a major contribution to the shaping of its image.

Daily newspaper mostly comment on political and economic developments, both domestic and international. Sports, crime and any odd happenings is grist to the editorial writer's will. Business newspaper, of which now there are quite a few in the country, naturally devote a major portion of their editorials to economic and financial subjects and these tend to be specialised. Weeklies and other magazines ensure that their comment do not become outdated until the next issues is out.

(ii) Importance of Editorials

Ans. It is the expression of an opinion in concise, logical terms, an interpretation of happenings to make their significance clear to the reader. It can be a combination of facts and opinion, for facts sometimes have to be given to justify opinion. One of the best definition is offered by M. Lyle Spencer in his book Editorial Writing: "An editorial is an expression of fact and opinion in concise, logical, pleasing order for the sake of entertaining, of influencing opinion, or of interpreting significant news in such a way that its importance to the average reader will be clear."

There is a positive personal motivation in writing editorials. Although, editorial writers remain anonymous in today's newspapers but their long association with journalism makes them known even without a by line.

'The Press and America'. Edwin Emery says that in the 17th century the papers in the big U.S. cities often printed pamphlets concerned with political and social issues. These pamphlets were offered to readers through the papers. By 1800, the day of the pamphlet had very nearly passed, and the editorial had supplanted it. Joshep Pulitzer, the famous U.S. newspaper man, used editorials for public purposes and his campaigns. Through news items and editorials, of his paper **World**, Pulitzer inaugurated a series of public services. Christmas dinners for the poor, free ice for tenement dwellers in summer, a staff of 35 doctors to serve the needy, to raise money for placing the Status of Liberty in New York. The World's editorials were of boundless coverage and were free from all sorts of advertising domination.

In Britain the editor remained responsible for the entire contents of the paper and generally devoted a great deal of time to the editorials, in the United States the managing editor became responsible for news and the editorial page editor, the junior partner, for opinion.

In India, all reputed dailies have their editorial columns. The pre-occupation of newspapers with political developments is a legacy of the day of our freedom struggle, but in course of time, this has given way to a wider perspective embracing economic, social and international developments. Since politics plays a major part in national life, its importance is reflected in the newspaper editorial pages. Social issues steal the editorial highlight on benchmark occasions such as the eruption of a caste of communal conflict or the occurrence of some henious crime that shocks society. On such occasions, while presenting its views, the editor not only expresses his concern and anguish over the development, but also suggests remedies to prevent a recurrence of the problem.

(iii) Should Editorials always be Adversarial?

Ans. It has been a debate for long on whether a newspaper should take an adversarial role in relation to the government or should offers constructive criticism with regard to the government activities and policies as and when it requires. Many argue that the press should be the watchdog and stand for the people and welfare of the society. Inaugurating the centenary celebrations of the Kesari founded by Lokmanya Balgangadhar Tilak on January 14, 1981, late Prime Minister Indira Gandhi said that neither a statesman nor an editor could have the last word. "What interests me more is the relationship between newspapers and the people. If editors and correspondents write for the people rather than for those in politics, their own effectiveness will increase and they will be able to serve the public better." However, Lokmanya says the press should be "fearless and frank" in whatever they write.

(iv) Letters to Editor

Ans. No newspaper has advance knowledge of the readers' reaction to the information carried by it; the reactions follow the publication. The writers, journalists and editors, while writing any article, expect the readers to like the material and to get positive reactions. A letter to the editor is a written way of talking to a newspaper, magazine, or other regularly printed publication. Letters to the editor are generally found in the first section of the newspaper, or towards the beginning of a magazine, or in the editorial page. They can take a position for or against an issue, or simply inform, or both. They can convince readers by using emotions, or facts, or emotions and facts combined. Letters to the editor are usually short and tight, rarely longer than 300 words. These letters are related to various subjects. Various articles published in a newspaper carry different views and opinions; in a way, a newspaper is an open forum and the best medium to give vent to the public views and opinions on various subjects. This column is very helpful in the policy making of the newspaper; however, it must be understood that the policy of a newspaper cannot the readers' mind.

Though an editor enjoys wide discretion in the matter of selection of letters, readers enjoying certain locus stand on an issue should be allowed to air their views.

If in the opinion of an editor, an article or news items submitted for publication could be liable to legal proceedings or any future complications, its publication would rest on the discretion of the editor since it is he who is answerable for anything published in the paper.

The editorial is a journalistic essay, its title should aim to inform the reader about the subject of the editorial and arouse his interest. The simplest form of editorial structure is to state the subject and to comment to it. In writing an editorial, a pattern may be employed:

- the statement of the subject;
- the expansion of the subject by means of comment; and
- an application or conclusion drawn from the comment.

Q12. What is an editorial page? Discuss the process how to plan an editorial Page.

Ans. The editorial page is one place in the newspaper where opinion is not only permissible but encouraged. The editorial page is dominated by comment and analysis rather than objective reporting of factual information. Here, the opinions of the newspaper's editorial board are put forth in editorials. The editorial page is one place in the newspaper where opinion is not only permissible but encouraged. It is dominated by comment and analysis rather than objective reporting of factual information. An editorial page can be exciting, different and attractive. But success doesnot just happen. The entire page must be organised in advance.

As a rule, an editorial page contains no advertisement. In six or eight page papers, the facing page often contains more features material. If so, both pages must be planned together. In daily newspapers that carry more than 20 pages, the location of the editorial page may vary, but it is generally fixed and is the same in any given newspapers. Major city papers use the facing page for related feature material. The main goal of an editorial page is to furnish the reader with background information about the news of the day. Editorials serve this purpose by interpreting or explaining current events. Editorial cartoons, columns, news features, personality sketches, or letters to the editor are planned to contribute to a better understanding of current happenings. At the centre of the page is a light article, generally humorous, of human interest of informative. Since it in the middle of the editorial page, it is also known as "middle". Besides, letters to the editor are also accommodated on the edit page. If a newspaper has several editions such as The Times of India, the same editorials generally appear on the same position at all centres. This is essential for the overall personality of a newspaper, its image and for making an impact on a particular issue. However, it is not essential that in all editions of the same newspaper, everyone should carry the same editorials.

Numerous kinds of copy are appropriate for an editorial page. These are:

- **Editorials:** The entire page exists as a showcase for editorials. They are chosen and written with care, and are the central attraction of the page.
- **Editorial Cartoons:** When well conceived and illustrated, editorial cartoons share the spotlight with editorials and can influence the readers in the same manner.
- **News Features:** News features are the most useful stories in newspapers. They are equally at home on news page, sports page, or editorial page. Their variety in subject, approach, length and style gives them high reader appeal on the editorial page. Both entertaining and information news features should be used regularly.
- **Personalities:** Interview or personality stories attract interest on editorial page.
- **Letters to the Editor:** This feature is particularly appropriate for the editorials, and needs the same careful preparation.
- **Columns:** Other columns of all kinds are desirable editorial page material.
- **Views on the News:** Interpretation of news includes giving background information, presenting sidelights on news events, showing how several events are related, and providing editorial comment.
- **Reviews:** Reviews may be written about movies, books, art exhibits, plays, musical productions and other forms of entertainment.

- **Creative Writing:** The editorial page offers possibilities for occasional input of original creative literary efforts. Individuals, who prepare them, may not be staff members, because a different kind of literary ability is required for it.

Q13. Write the comments of Pt. Jawahar Lal Nehru on Editorial Freedom.

Ans. The first Prime Minister, Jawaharlal Nehru, whose speeches and writings educated a whole nation in the crucial days after independence, spoke of "freedom and licence" when he addressed the All-India Newspaper Editors Conference in New Delhi on December 3, 1950.

While upholding freedom of the press. Nehru asked the editors to remember that they had their obligations. He said: "We should have freedom by all means but we should try to maintain certain integrity of approach to public activities". He said that the daily dose of thought, regularly given by newspapers affected the reader's mind. If a reader is told to do this or that, he might resist; but the slight daily dose, if it is right can improve his mind and, if it is wrong, can corrupt him.

In his speech at another AINEC meeting on September 17, 1952, Nehru presented his thoughts on various aspects of the functioning of the press. He pointed out that newspapers function in a difficult atmosphere; they had to say something quickly and they had not much time to think. There was no reason why newspapers should not have some amount of leisured thinking and wisdom – if not always – in the leading articles.

Interestingly, that was an occasion when Nehru had a dig at newspapermen, delightfully comparing them to politicians. He said, "To some extent, politicians and newspapermen or journalists have much in common. Both presume to talk too much, to write too much, to deliver homilies. Both, generally speaking, require to qualifications at all for their job. It does not mean that no politician or newspaperman has any qualification". Nehru pointed out that for any average profession – medicine, engineering or any other, a person had to go through a long course of training. He must obtain his degrees and diplomas only then was he allowed to practice, but was not so with politicians and newspapermen.

Q14. Give the definition and characteristics of editorials. Also, discuss the types of Editorials.

Ans. An editorial may be defined as a journalistic essay which neither attempts (1) to inform or explain, (2) to persuade or convince, or (3) to stimulate insight in an entertaining or humourous manner. It has an introduction, a body and a conclusion. The editorial articles are also called "leaders". News interpretation and background articles are different from the editorials in that they do not seek to convey the editorial views on the subject.

Lester Markel, a famous Sunday editor of the New York Times had said: "What you see is news; what you know is background; what you feel is opinion."

According to Joseph Pulitzer, the famous editor, newspapers should be "both a dairy teacher and a daily tribune."

Newspaper also carry on their opinion pages from the contributions of columnists. The columnists are like lawyers presenting a particular point of view. One columnist might differ completely with another on the same subject and interpret the same development differently. Reading all shades of opinion on a major controversy would be helpful to the reader to arrive at his own conclusions and judgement.

Characteristics of the Editorials

- Addresses a subject that is timely and relevant to the intended audience
- Is concise and coherent (number of words may be limited by the publication)
- Captures the audience's attention immediately in the opening
- Expresses the writer's opinion clearly
- Includes specific details that support the opinion and meets the needs of the audience
- Answers potential questions the audience might have
- Conveys a thorough knowledge of the subject and correct information
- Follows an organizational plan that attracts the audience's attention
- Suggests a possible solution to the problem or issue addressed
- Avoids phrases such as I think, I believe, in my opinion, it seems to me, or I for one
- Maintains a courteous and polite tone

Types of Editorials: In a newspaper/magazine, editorials are not always written by the editor. Newspapers generally have a band of writers known as editorial writers, leader writers or assistant editors to write editorials. Most of these writers are specialists in various subjects such as disarmament, UN agencies, economics, international affairs, education, science, media, literature and law. An editorial writer writes the editorial piece as per the style and policy of the newspaper.

Editorials can be classified in different ways. On the basis of its purpose, it can be informative, argumentative or entertaining. On the basis of its form of composition, it may be narrative, descriptive or expository. An editorial can also be classified on the basis of its contents. Thus, it can be political, social, economic, historical and scientific. Further editorials can be grouped under local, national, regional and international.

Interpretative and explanatory editorials expand the dimension of the news reports. Editorial writers keep in mind the requirements of a reader when they write the editorial. In most Indian newspaper the general length of an editorial is between 300 and 400 words. If the editorial pieces are longer than this reader may not have the time or patience unless they are of gripping interest.

An argumentative editorial tries to convince the reader about its point of view. Such editorials aim to influence and mould public opinion. Editorial writers use logic and techniques of propaganda to fulfill the objectives.

Newspapers also write editorials to take note or a major development. For instance, if an earthquake or an air crash in a distant country has caused the loss of a large number of lives, the Editor sympathises with the victims. A train accident or an air crash in one's own country on the other hand would involve an analysis of the factors that caused the accident, finding out whether any one was at fault and a critical of the authorities responsible for running the service.

Newspaper also write editorials that amuse and entertain. Such pieces are usually published as the third edit by major English newspapers. Humour adds to their appeal for the reader whose interests are not confined to politics and economics. Subjects for editorials include the fickle weather, innocent faux pass committed by those in authority, any unusual incident or literary controversies. The editorial writer should have has in-depth knowledge about the subjects of general interest or on the subject he is writing about.

Q15. Define Policy, Style and Guidelines in Editorial Writing.

Ans. Editorials follow the policy of the newspaper while the articles contributed by the writers outside do not adopt the policy of the newspaper. The edit page articles are meant to broaden the horizon of news and opinion coverage. The articles are generally of 12,00 to 18,00 words. Some of them combine in themselves the presentation of facts as well as opinion. Some articles are useful as backgrounders. The cartoon is also a sort of opinion piece. While the cartoonist cannot violate editorial policy, he enjoys a wide latitude in depicting big personalities as ordinary men and punching the balloon of lofty statements.

The Press Council has also laid down some principles in the regard. Some of them are given below:

- Sensational headlines with incorrect innuendos must be avoided as they lend an unethical character to publications. Editors should verify facts before publishing any article which is likely to damage the reputation of a person, organization or institution.
- Newspaper/magazine editorials should not use filthy, scurrilous or irresponsible comments.
- Any comment against the government or any person must be based on information. It must be checked and verified from authentic sources. Even after verification, the comments should be presented in decent, dignified and restrained language.
- Editorials conceived in bad taste bordering on scurrility and with a motive to denigrate, cannot be said to by good ones and should be avoided.
- Newspaper should never publish fabricated or concocted story as it is gross impropriety for a newspaper to publish such a story, and also in editorial on it.
- Contradiction pertaining to defamatory articles containing personal allegations should be published promptly with due prominence.

Q16. What is the difference between an Editorial and other Newspaper Writings?

Ans. There are several different types of newspaper writings, each focusing on a unique subject. For example, a sports article would focus on a sporting event, whereas a feature article would focus on culture or film. The distinction between an editorial and a news article, however, can be the center of some confusion. A broad rule to live by is to remember that an editorial is structured around an opinion, while a news article focuses entirely around a factual news story.

Editorial Pieces: The editorial piece is written by a senior staff member of a publication that traditionally appears in the opinion section of the periodical. They are typically unsigned and are meant to represent the views and opinions of the periodicals in which they appear. Occasionally, they may be accompanied with photographs or artwork relating to the theme or topic of the piece. The editorial board of a publication dictates what subject the piece will focus on; these are usually subjects that relate to the reader's community or life. Editorial cartoons are also considered to be a form of the editorial piece.

These opinionated pieces appear "opposite the editorial page," hence the common op-ed abbreviation. While an editorial piece is written from a staff member of the publication, an op-ed piece is typically written by someone unaffiliated with the periodical. Pieces can be written on any topic that the writer has a strong opinion about. The writer is given a byline (authorship), and can directly oppose the views of the editorial board. Ultimately, the editor decides whether or not the piece will appear in the publication.

Historical Editorial: This form focuses on an event that happened. Historical editorials may offer a different view of history, or challenge a preconceived notion of a particular event. Furthermore, they can offer a firsthand account of a significant moment in history. For example, an opinion piece written by a survivor of the 9/11 attacks would offer a first-hand account of the tragic event. Like the copied pieces, they feature a named writer.

News Articles: Stories about actual happenings and events without a personal bias or opinion are considered to be news articles. They strictly outline the who, what, where, when and why of an event. These appear in the news section of the periodical, on the front page of a newspaper. For example, a news story about 9/11 would explain the people involved, the number of casualties and the circumstances of the tragedy.

Q17. Discuss the concept and increased scope of a freelance writer.

Ans. Several persons write articles, reviews, features, on all kinds of topics. Some of them write in several newspapers, and periodicals, day in and day out, though they are not on the regular payrolls of these newspapers and magazines. They are known as 'Freelance Writers'. Generally speaking, freelance journalists are not attached to any newspaper or magazines. Most magazines and periodicals depends a lot on these freelancer, for making these publications interesting and for meeting the reading needs of all kinds of readers.

Freelancers quite frequently keep in touch with magazines, and do assignments as per their needs. With a view of meeting their needs, freelancers have to complete these assignments as per the schedules of the publication. The origin of freelancing is believed to go back to the 16th century when freelancers were associated with military life. A lancer or the person who wielded swords was free and his allegiance was limited to a particular assignment for which he was hired. From the 16th to 18th centuries, several such freelancers came to India from Europe to train the armies of Tipu Sultan, the Marathas and the Newabs of Bengal. They even fought for their armies but never went to the camps of the opponent or betrayed the temporary masters. Their masters kept a watchful eye on them but never found them lacking. They were found thoroughly dependable. This is what a freelance writer has to be.

Increased Scope for Freelancers: Magazine journalism now-a-day is not much different from newspaper journalism. Both delve in facts. The television is also making a difference to it. Television news is forcing newspapers into a new culture of dealing with the items more thoroughly. Newspapers closely resemble magazines.

For a freelance writer the scope is vast. The onslaught of television has spurred in the scope for freelance writing. The magazines and newspapers are now keener on giving more graphic details. They are in need of more absorbing contents. This also enlarges opportunities for any freelancer. A real good writer can even get a chance to write scripts for various television programmes. To develop into a good writer, that is, an acceptable contributor to periodicals, there is a need to read various magazines and newspapers and understand what kind of stuff they use. We just cannot churn out anything that we like but we should know what our readers like. Occasionally, perhaps what we have written without giving a thought may be accepted by an editor, but more often that is not the case. We may face more rejection slips than acceptance. To avoid rejection, a proper planning, research and a list of users – is a must. As an unattached writer or a freelancer, we cannot depend only on one user. There must be alternatives. We have to gradually build up contacts with magazines and newspapers to be accepted as a freelancer.

Q18. Discuss who can be a Freelance Writer.

Ans. A freelance writer is someone who writes without belonging to any single company or entity but acts like a small business or an independent contractor. It's possible to be a full-time freelance writer earning a living, or to be a part-time freelancer supplementing a regular income. Virtually anybody can be a freelance writer. Most freelance writers, actually, have other jobs. A typical freelancer gives only a part of his energy and writing talent to this type of writing. Many leading novelists and short story or article writers who contribute to magazines, or editorial pages of newspapers, are university teachers, housewives, staff members publications houses or book companies, lawyers, doctors, etc. who are largely engaged in some other occupations or profession other than writing.

All freelancers have gone through it at some point of time. If we want to see our name in print, we must not lose heart. All writers, be they on the staff, or freelancers, have seen their pieces being rejected at one time or the other for various reasons. All this does not mean that a writer who wishes to contribute to publications cannot hope someday to reach the point where he has to do no other work. But it is difficult to make writing a full-time occupation, especially in the realm of fiction. For, the market for the short poetry, story, novelette and novel is not as great among magazines as it was some three decades ago. Today, there is more chance for the non-fiction writer—the author of articles on current subjects, humorous essays, and other factual rather than imagined material.

(1) Freelancers Receive Rejections: The percentage of accepted material is very small. At the same time, any magazine editor's common complaint is that they do not receive enough good stuff. It is a painful job for the editor to reject a piece. He just does not reject something because he does not like the name of a person or the subject on which he has written. The reasons for over 90 per cent of rejections is just one language does not make a piece good. There has to be some originality, specificity and exclusiveness, in the piece that a writer sends for acceptance.

Quite often, people write on topics on which the writer does not know enough. They lift one para from here and the other from there, to churn out a piece. Else, they try to rewrite a piece they have read somewhere and try to pass it as original. In yet another case, they choose good topics, neither do they study it, not do appropriate research which is so necessary to make a piece readable or absorbing. Some people would write on any subject. Today they may be writing on science, tomorrow on cinema or arts and a day after on information technology. Editors do not like such writers. By chance one or two of their pieces will get published because possibly the editor has a pressing deadline to meet or he had nothing better on hand. We cannot be jack or all trades.

(2) Freelancing as a Side Business: An ambitious freelance writer should consider his work as part-time or side business, i.e. in addition to his other full-time jobs or profession. It has to remain an extra-curricular activity while he devotes years to becoming an expert in a specialized area. Even after gaining a reputation, he will find it necessary to retain permanent connections with institutions in the special field, to provide a support for his creativity. Most freelancers depend upon their principal vacation not only for their regular income, but also as a source of facts and ideas. No freelancer can function in a vacuum. Anything he sees and does has possibilities for an article.

Q19. Discuss about freelance writer that what he can write.

Ans. A freelance writer can write on any subject. Broadly, acceptable freelance contributions can be divided into the following categories:

(1) Article: An article is like an essay. But, it is not an essay as it is less personal and less limited in scope. It is a written composition of variable length, intended to convey ideas and facts for the purpose of informing, educating, enlightening, convincing, instructing or entertaining. There is no exact set of rule for how to begin an article. Generally, it can begin with a catchy introduction to attract the reader, and then ideas and facts may be interestingly intertwined. Articles can be written on umpteen subjects - plain facts that may be unknown, new ideas to mould a project or schemes like the Narmada Sagar Project, economy, science and technology, fashion designing, rural urban, semi-rural, semi-urban and rural-urban features, etc.

(2) Features: Features are often linked to current events. Feature writers are often captivated by their own graceful writing, letting their skill overshadow the fact that they are linked closely to the news. As a feature writer, he has to learn to recognize that his proper positioning is half way between news story and the feature. Good feature stories are always in great demand. Unusual hobbies like having a lion as a pet, success stories, as it was in the case of GeetSethi, who was brought into the limelight by a sports feature writer, who was able to not only point out his victory but also how it almost went unnoticed in the Indian media and how he returned to the Bombay airport almost unsung. Inventions—recently one newspaper carried the breakthrough by Indian Institute of Technology scientists in the sphere of developing cryogenic rocket technology: interviews, personality stories and human interest stories—all can be turned into good features.

(3) Reviews/Analyses: There are many events which can neither be a feature nor an article. Evaluating or even descriptive pieces can be written about music, drama, ballet or such other cultural performances. Such writing, can be termed review pieces. There is yet another kind of review. This is associated with books. A large number of books are published day in and day out. If we are a keen reader, we can get in touch with some of the book section editors of magazines or newspapers and can get the books in which we have comparative specialization. This is a real bonus for us. A book reviewer is not only paid a good sum, but is also allowed to retain the book he has reviewed. While reviewing, we need not summarise the books contents. It needs an expert evaluation and the reader has to be told what kind of a book it is. We must avoid writing whether it is good or bad.

An analysis examines in detail an issue. This can be an evaluation of a scientific work or of a building project. But remember, whatever it is, it must have something novel in it. It can be even a controversy. Any newspaper or magazine is unlikely to accept any analysis. It will accept only if there is something new to add to what the newspaper/magazine has already published about it. State matters do not sell and such stuff makes a periodical all the more unreadable. An analysis should be argumentative and deal with the pros and cons of an issue.

Q20. Give some tips on how to become a successful freelancer.

Ans. The first step to successful freelance writing is to understand what it is exactly that we are getting into. Though most periodicals and newspapers accept manuscripts by mail, it has been observed that those writers who establish a personal rapport with editors are more successful in seeing their work in print. A good public relation is always helpful.

There is yet another reason for this. Often, freelancers leave many queries in their copy. A face to face encounter helps editors solve these. In the course of time, if an editor likes the pieces, he may also ask to write on topics or issue in which he is interested. So many kind of information pour in the newspaper offices and editor gets news ideas out of these. Once the editor is assured of competence, he may start depending on a freelancer.

For example, a teacher who in his leisure, studied films. He saw all news movies. Being a member of the film society, he got many new ideas and stories, about movies. In the beginning, he used to rush with his reviews to newspapers and magazines. In the course of time, his work was linked by some editors. Now, his column appears almost every week. Recently, he was given the best film journalist's awards. We must have realised that besides being a good writer, we should have a good rapport with our editors. This is all the more possible if we are living in a metropolis or large centres of publication. But if we are living in a far off place, we need not lose heart. We can send our copy by mail. If it has been written in the style of a magazine or newspaper, there is a fair chance that our copy will be accepted.

It is also prudent to send self-addressed stamped envelopes with our manuscript. The rejected manuscript will come back to us. We can send it to some other publication who may use it. To be successful freelancer, we ought to have patience.

If we are writing in English, always send typewritten manuscripts. Editors are averse in accepting handwritten articles. It involves a lot of additional work, like getting the copy typed and then editing it. It means loss of time. An editor, who has to work against deadlines, cannot afford to lose time. For him, the easiest way out is to reject a handwritten copy. In case, we are writing in a regional language, again, the same rule holds good. But as there are fewer language typewriters, and editors are in need of good stuff, handwritten copy is also accepted. However, write neatly and legibly and only on one side of the paper.

Q21. Discuss the concept of magazine writing. Also, write its types.

Ans. In the early days, magazines in India started in different languages to provide opportunities to creative talents. The Modern in India Review was one such publication. The concept of a news magazine was developed in India. The Illustrated Weekly of India, not only gave literary inputs, but also published articles and features about varied experiences and gave detailed coverages of news events. The Time magazine of the USA, which the Link magazine in India tired to follow, gave a new dimension to magazine journalism. These magazines not only gave features, analysis, culture and book reviews, but also comments on the political and economic developments and many other area. The magazine attempted to provide a complete picture with comments on the events of the week that had gone by.

The term "magazine" was used as part of the name of a publication in 1731, when it went into the title of the Gentleman's Magazines of London. The application was suitable, for the word comes from the French "magazine", which means storehouse. The early magazines in England were storage places for sketches, verse, essays and miscellaneous writings on variety of subjects.

In earlier years, the term had to do with contents and not with the format. Thus, a publication with a newspaper format with a wide variety of content was considered a magazine. The magazine, as opposed to the newspaper, made no effort to print up the minute news, but tried to present fiction, travel articles and other materials for entertainment. There are general appeal magazines such as the Reader's Digest and its multi-language multiple-million editions with worldwide circulation. These are, however, becoming exceptions in India. The mortality rate of magazines in India has been rather high though new ones are also coming up with dexterous regularity. The decline in circulation is attributed to the boom in television programmes, lack of time to read and, the Sunday multi-color supplement of the daily newspaper.

Types of Magazine

- **Consumer general interest:** India Today, Frontline, the Week and Sunday in India, Reader's Digest, Newsweek and Time in the US.
- **Specialised:** Business journals mentioned above, Technical journals, Indian Historical Quarterly, Indian Archaeology, Science Reporter, Farm Review: Indian Architecture, Marg (on arts).
- **There are also magazines for elites:** Gentleman, Debonair, Society, Women, Femina, Women's Era, Savvy, body & beauty

Care, Fashion, Dress Designing; and also on behavioral aspects – wildlife and exploration like National Geographic of the US.

Q22. Write short notes on the following

(i) Freelancing for magazines

Ans. Given below are some tips for those who are freelancing for magazine:

- Choose a subject, and do a lot of reading on it from a variety of sources – journals, magazines, reference books.
- Draw outlines from the notes after readings from several sources.
- Write a lead, build around re-organised ideas and decide whether an anecdote would be fitting to precede the lead.
- In one sitting, try to write 1,000 to 1,500 words non-stop. The writing must have depth and background. Try to develop only one idea at a time. Other ideas can emerge into another article or a separate feature.
- Be selective. Don't try to put in all the knowledge into one piece. Don't make it a dumping ground. Spice it selectively. Omit less important or not so relevant details. Too many facts or figures make it an uninteresting reading, and a loaded write-up.
- After completing the article, forget about it for a day or two. Then, again re-read it like a dispassionate and critical reader. In all likelihood, we would be able to make out where our piece is jarring, disjointed and has other flaws.

(ii) Cultivate keen Observation Faculty

Ans. Freelance writer can generate ideas with keen observation during travelling by a long distance train, while visiting a place or attending to a patient in a hospital. We can see the change in complexion of its passengers as it traverses different regions. At the end of the journey, our experience with some of our fellow passengers can be an interesting story. We also write about our experience in a hospital. Sit and jot down the points and that can be developed into beautiful write-ups.

- **Article Ideas from PR Persons:** Public Relations persons are generally passive journalists. They move in a wide circle and come to know so many things. If we develop a friendship with such persons, they can suggest story topics to us that are not self-serving. For a journalist to ignore all such Public Relations persons or treat their suggestions cynically is unfair. A good article remains a good product even if it benefits the person who gives such ideas. We need only to guard against being used for unworthy purposes.

- **Article Ideas from Editors:** As we establish ourselves and begin to write regularly for a magazine or a periodical, we can expect our editor to begin suggesting topics to us to develop. In due course of time, half of our ideas can come from editors.

(iii) How Freelance Writing Works

Ans. A freelance writer is not attached to any newspaper, organization; Nor is he on the payroll. The confidence in the editor has to be instilled. Indeed, to develop into a credible and dependable freelance writer needs not only skill but also some conviction. He cannot promise a write-up to one magazine or newspaper and then sell it to the other higher bidder. Nor is he normally supposed to give his articles or features for publication simultaneously to more than one publication. Only a syndicated writer can do this.

Q23. Describe some ideas for magazine articles.

Ans. We can get an idea for a write-up from anywhere, but it is not that easy to write for magazine if we are beginner. Of course, an experienced person can generate ideas simply by setting his mind to the task. A newcomer in the field will find it difficult to do that. Here are two ideas for magazine articles for beginners given below:

(1) Ideas for College Campus: The college or the university campus can be an excellent source of ideas and information for articles. College or university students union or teachers' association elections or senate meetings always generate heat and interest in the local community. A systematic and simple description can make an enjoyable piece. Groupism among teachers in favour of or against the head of the institution, or a tip off about some new appointments can also make a good story. Even as simple a thing as announcement or shifting of examination dates spiced with the reason behind it can be of interest to the local paper.

(2) Search Ideas from Newspaper Columns: Anyone who wants to become a freelancer should read his daily newspaper carefully. There are a number of small news events which can be developed into articles of features. If the journalist had not had the knack, that innocuous piece of news would have, just been lost into oblivion. The writer must read and analyse magazines to get a feel what kind of articles it published. Read as many newspapers as possible for ideas. We must see more than the facts. We should also be able to see their implications.

Freelancer can use company journals or house magazines which are sometimes heavy with facts, they can be used profitably by freelancers. University magazines and research journals which are also rich sources of materials, are usually available free to a writer and can be obtained regularly through the mail. Similarly, annual official reports also provide a storehouse of ideas.

Q24. How do we build an Article? Give the guidelines.

Ans. It is very important that our writing is clear and readable on whatever topic or subject we are writing. Some of the guidelines are given below, this will make our writing clear and readable:

- **Story Structure:** The beginners are told that a lead must catch and hold their readers. The lead is the introduction or intro, in journalistic parlance. If possible, the intro should be startling, witty or a pithy statement. Do not try to devote the beginning to summing up a story, much as straight news story often does.
- **Sentence Structure:** Beginners generally like to twist their sentences. We should do this rarely, for effect. The normal rule is that nearly all sentences should be as simple and direct as possible.
- **Sentence Length:** As a rule, we must keep our sentences short. Generally, the shorter the sentence, the more readable it will be. Have you read My Experiments with Truth by Mahatma Gandhi? Do it. We will notice how simple and effective the Mahatma's sentences are.
- **Concreteness:** As far as possible, we should use concrete words instead of abstract ones. Abstract words confuse as reader and that is considered bad for an article and a feature story.
- **Verb:** Making the verb do the work of an adjective is preferable. The verb expresses action. If it is carefully chosen, it can even describe personality. "The magazine gives description" can be written: "The magazine described". This not

only economises on words, but also makes the expression accurate.

- **Transitions:** Learning to link paragraphs in a way that pull that reader on is a skill that distinguishes the professional from the amateur. After the first paragraph, what comes next – we have to learn. This we can do by reading special pages of India Today, Reader's Digest, Time, Newsweek or Sunday. The literary pages of The Statesman are also a good guide.

Q25. Define the role of style for magazine article.

Ans. A writer is known by his own style. Every writer writes is his own way. Some are humorous and light, some serious and observant and some are analytical. A beginner cannot be expected to develop such a style over-night. But when we consider style and content, the focus sharpens.

Magazine writing is a distinct body of prose; usually made up of words the readers can under-stand and information he can absorb. Vivid writing should be spicy but one must restrain himself as dictated by taste and common sense The general style followed by most magazines consists of crisp, original phrases made up of familiar words. Pointed quotations are sprinkled through most articles to change the pace to enliven the reading and to present facts distinctively. The writing flows from the starting to the end through smooth transition. If is a profile, do not start with a bland statement on such and such day. Start with some of the qualities or starting deed and then gradually we can mention these points.

- **Sticking to the Theme:** There should be only one main theme. Do not deviate from it.
- **One Story at a Time:** Do not try to juxtapose too many ideas into one story. This makes piece disjointed and the reader (read editor) becomes disinterested.
- **Make it Vivid:** Give a detailed and interesting description. But these should be so short that it should not deviate from the main theme. Too much spice spoils a dish. Writer has to remember this.
- **Fiction is not Journalism:** Beginner should know that journalism is different from fiction. A fiction is an imaginary piece which may or may not have drawn its inspiration from a

real life event. The fiction writer mixes a product of the imagination with facts. Fiction is fabrication. Journalism on the other hand is concerned with facts. The market form fiction magazine writing has gradually been reduced. Sometimes some magazines publish fiction, but most do not.

Q26. Discuss the future for freelancing.

Ans. The onslaught of television has made a dent in the circulation magazines. At the same time, it has expected magazine publishers to be more conscious about quality. The production has become more attractive than a decade or so ago. With growing education the yearning to know more about a specific field is rising. The competition is also comparatively less for a specialised magazine. These factors are destined to grow in the years to come. As a freelancer, we have a better chance to grow as a specialised writer. In fact, specialised writers are even now in great demand and it is bound to go up in the future. Politics tempts, but remember this is one area on which many people write and publications accept articles only from the veterans in the field.

The relationship between the writer and editor is based on trust. An editor expects the writer to remain loyal to him in a limited sense. He does not expect to send the written piece to other. If the writer does even once, he loses his trust and loses the market.

If we are writing for feature or article syndicates, our write-up may get simultaneously published in several magazines. The syndicates multiply the copy and send it to different publications at a time. The writer is paid by the syndicate a percentage of the total sum it receives from the publication. The syndicates and publications have some sort of arrangement about supplying material. Publications, however, are under no compulsion to use these. They can, if they need it or like it. As a freelancer, syndicates also offer us enough opportunities.

Some common ethical points that should follow for our guidelines are as follows:

- **Truthfulness and Accuracy:** The main responsibility is the information in the write-up should be based on the facts. There should not be any manipulation of facts.
- **Rewriting:** A beginner's copy is often rewritten. But an experienced writer frowns at this practice. If some copy is very badly written, the editor may ask him to rewrite it or would do

so with permission of the writer. If the publication of a piece has been delayed, the editor can ask the writer to update it.

- **By-lines:** A by-line is the author's unquestioned right.
- **Payment:** A writer should have the surety that he is paid for his write-up on time. Normally, once an article is accepted, it is the obligation of the publication to make the payment. But, there are many publications which do not.

4 WRITING FOR RADIO AND TELEVISION

INTRODUCTION

A radio news story is written for the ear, it is not meant for reading. A radio story is also not for any particular segment of the society. It is neither targeted for any special ethnic group nor is limited to any geographical boundary. Its drafting is therefore more ticklish than the print or visual media. The most important stylistic principle in radio news writing is simplicity. If the language is too complex, it is possible that the story will not be completely understood by the audience. The radio listener cannot retrieve lost information by reading a sentence or story. If the story is not understood the first time around, it would be lost to the listener forever. Radio news writers generally apply a few rules of their own to help them get information across in the best (simplest form): keep the sentence short, avoid complex sentences or construction and use basic words not colloquialisms. Television news style is much like radio news style, for a viewer can no more return to a group of facts than a listener can. The viewer, like the listener, does not always focus on what the newscaster says. Television news adds further complexities when pictures join the words; that is, anchors or reporters deliver what is called a "voiceover."

Q1. Make a Structure of News Services Division of All India Radio (AIR).

Ans. The News Services Division (NSD) of All India Radio disseminates news and comments to listeners in India and abroad. From 27 news bulletins in 1939-40, AIR today puts out 647 bulletins daily around 56 hours in 90 languages/dialects in the Home, Regional and External Services. Out of these, 178 bulletins are broadcast daily from Delhi in 33 languages. The 45 Regional News Units (RNUs) put out 469 daily news bulletins in 75 languages. This includes 314 headlines bulletins mounted on FM 'Rainbow' and from 40 AIR Stations. In addition to the daily news bulletins, the News Services Division also mounts number of news-based programmes on topical subjects from Delhi and its Regional News Units.

Air's News Services Division is headed by the Director General News, who is assisted by four Additional Directors General and seven Directional Officers (Joint Directors). They supervise the functioning of the General News Room, Reporting Units, Current Affairs Units, Language Units, Regional News Units and the Monitoring Service. The last mentioned service monitors broadcasts by foreign radio stations and makes them available to AIR.

Beside from receiving news from news agencies, AIR has over a hundred regular correspondents in the state capitals and other important centres. It also has 232 district-level part-time correspondents spread all over the country. Besides, there are seven Special Correspondents posted abroad.

(1) The Functioning of Radio News Room: Air receives three to four lakh words of news item during a 24 hour period. It is the responsibility of the news editors of AIR working in the General News Room in Delhi to examine this copy and select the usable items.

The Editor-in-Charge oversees the operation in every shift. He is assisted by a number of Editors.

They carefully read the selected news items and rewrite and reduce them as per the merits of the story. The longest radio bulletins, of 15 minutes duration, can only carry a little over 1500 words. Radio editors summarize an eight-or-ten page newspaper into just one page. Brevity is the hallmark of radio news bulletins.

Q2. Discuss about compilation of news of All India Radio news service.

Ans. Radio has added more responsibility on the shoulders of a newspaper reporter. Superficial coverage will not do now. The reporter will have to go deep into the subject and give as comprehensive coverage as possible.

In the general news room of All India Radio, editors select the news items which can be used and turned broadcast language. The copy testing is done by the editor in-charge and he passes on the selected items to other editors who turn it into what is called 'pool' copy. This 'pool' is circulated to all bulletin editors who select items according to the importance and the target audience.

(1) Pool Copy: The AIR News Room in New Delhi feeds news for some 146 Home and External news bulletins. To meet requirement, AIR has introduced a system that is called "news pool", which is prepared in English. All incoming news, after editing, is put into the pool which is split into news categories such as Home, Foreign, Parliament and Sports. Inclusion of an item in the pool means: (i) the news which is broadcast worthy, (ii) it has already been written in broadcast style and (iii) any linkages and back grounding required has been done.

The entire pool copy is distributed among all editors compiling different bulletins. Home, Regional and External. The editors preparing the pool copy also look after the important developing stories and constantly go on revising and updating them. They also prepare round ups of important events and happening such as riots, floods, disturbances and whatever is in the news.

The News Room has four shifts during a day and each shift issues its own pool copy, during morning, day time, evening and night. Compiling editors working on the language bulletins look after a group of bulletins like languages of East and South India. Similarly, the external bulletins are also combined.

(2) Compiling News Bulletins: Further, the compiling editors select and prune the news items, keeping in view the duration of each bulletin and the interest of the target audience. They prepare the bulletins and, together with the headlines, send them to the Language Units and the External Services Units where they are translated and put out in their languages.

Translation of news bulletins in different languages should not be mere transliteration. These should be re-written keeping in view the diction, style and flow of the language into which the translation is done. Also, the format of the language bulletins should be different.

(3) Selecting the Headlines: When the bulletin is prepared, the Editor decides which items apart from the lead story are to be headlined. Generally, the Editor selects headlines keeping in view the interest of the listeners. All bulletins have different headlines. The headlines given for Urdu bulletin will not the same for Oriya bulletin.

Headlines should be brief and written in simple language. These are generally repeated because quite often many listeners tune in late and only from the repeat headlines do they know the important news of the day. All items which figure in the headlines must be included in the bulletin. Sentences that are read after the headlines must give details about the main news items.

(4) Use of Spoken Language in the News Bulletins on Radio: As the news on the radio moves fast without the facility of recall which is possible, though, in the case of newspapers whatever is broadcast must be clear, precise and to the point. Sentences should be and direct without sub clauses. Brevity is essential as a minute broadcast time can take about 100 words, thus giving an editor the choice of about 1000 to 1100 words (in a 10-minute news bulletin) to cover world, national and regional news. There is a great constraint of space in radio, hence broadcast news must be big and important should be put in crisp and easily understood language. Ceremonial items or didactic speeches distract the attention of the listener who can always switch off or change over to some other programme.

(5) Clarity through the use of simple words: There should be no need for a dictionary while listening to a radio bulletin. It should be in words which are common in everyday speech. For example, "The work has started" and not "the work has commenced", "The play has ended" and not "terminated". There is no place for "officialese" in bulletins (officialese is the language used in officials press notes). The words chosen should create visual images in the mind. "Roads are under water" or "The telegraph poles have been uprooted" or "The bridges have been washed away" sound better than "The communications have been disrupted". Words like "hospitalised or "minimised" have no place in a radio bulletin. Instead say "admitted into the hospital" or "reduced to a minimum."

(6) Short Sentences: Never use long sentences in radio bulletin. Do not use long sentences. Avoid subordinate clauses; they are rarely used in every day conversation. The attention of an average radio listener cannot be held for long: so the sentences as well as the paragraphs have to be short. Avoid a sentence which is longer than 18 to 20 words. Otherwise, most listeners will not be able to follow it. So, the best thing to do is to split the long sentences. We must always put only one idea into one sentence.

The news items to be broadcast on radio also have to be short, generally not more than 90 or 100 words an item. Some items can be even shorter. Long items carrying ministerial speeches can only bore the listeners. It requires the mature, professional competence of a good radio or TV editor or reporter to pick up news points the ministerial speeches and make crisp items out of them.

(7) Present Tense: The present tense should be used wherever it is possible. Broadcasts on radio should appear to the listener to be happening at that moment. Instead of saying, "The new generator has been switched on". Instead of saying, "The Prime Minister said today that the country's economy is booming" write "The Prime Minister says the country's economy is booming". Editors of radio news do not bother too much about rules of written English. They always opt for the spoken language. Too many figures should not be given in radio news. These only confuse the listeners. Where figures become necessary, round them off. Instead of saying , "398,879,968" say "about 40 crores".

Q3. Define the role of Gatekeepers and Credibility in compiling, editing and presenting news.

Ans. For a long time, gatekeeping has provided a dominant paradigm for journalistic news gathering and news publishing in the mass media, both for journalists' own conceptualisation of their work and for academic studies of this mediation process. In media such as print, radio, and TV, with their inherent strictures of available column space, air time, or transmission frequencies, it is necessary to have established mechanisms which police these gates and select events to be reported according to specific criteria of newsworthiness, such as Galtung & Ruge's news values (1965).

In the news on radio, the reporters and editors are the 'gatekeepers'. They make important decisions about whether or not a news item shall be reported and also carried on air. Speed is of essence in radio news. The deadlines are much sharper than in the newspapers. With the introduction of hourly news bulletins, any item which is more than 60 minutes old might not be fresh. Consequently, reporting and editing for the radio calls for skills and speed. Events need to the reported as they take place to meet the first available news bulletins, developing stories need to be covered repeatedly adding fresh bits.

(1) Role of Bulleting Editors: A bulletin editor prepares the 15-minute main English news bulletin for the evening. On a given working day, a bulletin editor in the evening may have 45 to 50 items to consider from the day and evening shifts. They will include Home and Foreign news, Parliament news if Parliament is in session and Sports news. The items vary in length, say from 50 to 150 words. Some may even be of 200 words or more.

A 15-minute bulletin can carry only 1,500 to 1,600 words. This can vary depending on the newsreader who is reading news that evening. The pace of reading varies among newsreaders. This means that we will have to leave out less important items of the 'day pool' which will have gone in the day bulletins and further reduce the evening items.

Preparing the News Bulletin: There is no hard and fast rule. Generally, home stories are given preference. But if there is some foreign news, for example the death of a foreign VIP, overthrow of any foreign government, or a major air disaster naturally that becomes the lead. If there are other important foreign stories that day, they can go in the first bunch and the home stories can come in the second and the third bunch or "breaks" as they are called in the newsroom. A "break" in a bulletin comes after about five minutes and is meant to give a little pause, which gives welcome rest to the newsreader as well as prepares the listener for more news to follow. Generally, editors prefer to end the bulletin with sports news or with a human interest story.

(2) Role of Radio Reporters in News, Interviews and Commentaries: All radio organisations subscribe to news agencies. But the main subscribers of news agencies are newspapers. So, the news agency copy is done in newspaper style and has to be redone for use in radio bulletins. A radio organisation needs its own correspondents to do stories in the radio so that these can go straight into the bulletins. Radio reporters keep radio bulletin timings in mind and work to meet their deadlines. Air has thus regular correspondents and special correspondents posted abroad. It has also part time correspondents. Besides, all radio organisations also subscribe to news agencies. But agency copies need to be rewritten for the bulletin.

(i) **Voice Dispatch:** Apart from giving scripted stories, an important part of a radio reporter's job is to give voice dispatches which have become an essential part of radio bulletins in the developed countries. The purpose of a voice dispatch in the correspondent's voice is to supplement, add colour and authenticity to the basic news. An eye-witness account or an on-the-spot report complete with background sound can be very convincing. Writing a voice report is different from writing straight news. In a voice report, we can add something to the news that is more personal.

(ii) **Interviews and Commentaries:** Radio reporters and even editors often have to do interviews for news or news-related programmes such as Radio Newsreel, or commentaries such as Spotlight and Current Affairs Programmes. Unlike newspaper interviewers, radio reporters must have a clear idea of the duration of the recorded interview they want to have with an author, an actor or artist or a politician. They should be able to brief the interviewees about it in advance. The questions have to be brief and pointed; one question at a time. The interviewer has to carefully listen to the answers and then follow them up with further questions. The interviewer must learn to put searching questions without being offensive.

(ii) **Credibility:** Radio news report should give a total picture, the good and the bad, whether it is about a project, a factory, a strike, a VIP visit or anything else. The listener will like to have an unbiased picture. It is this fairness and accuracy in news and other programmes which gives credibility to a radio organisation.

It is true that the electronic media in India and other developing countries are still under government control. In India, the Prasar Bharati law has been passed by Parliament. The Act provides for the electronic media being entrusted to an Autonomous Corporation. But whether the electronic media remain directly under the government or are entrusted to an autonomous corporation, the quality of their programmes will essentially depend on the professional competence of the staff, editors, reporters and producers. Also, their ability to stand up against pressures and produce their programmes fairly and fearlessly. It is only by doing this that radio and television organisations all over the world have become increasingly autonomous in their functioning and earned the respect and admiration of their audiences.

During the past 60 years or more, radio in India has been playing an important role as a medium to educate, entertain and inform the people. It has promoted arts, literature and drama. Even in the field of agriculture, it made a significant contribution by propagating an improved variety of rice. It has also been covering all crises, such as wars with Pakistan and China, or floods or drought. The radio thus has provided timely information through its news bulletins and other programmes.

Q4. Write short notes on the followings:

(i) Types of News Bulletins

Ans. On the audience profile AIR broadcast three types of bulletin - one for overseas audience, second for national and third is for regional. The External Service Division looks after the news bulletins to be broadcast abroad. Both English and Hindi bulletins are broadcast on the national network. Some news bulletins in the regional languages are also broadcast from Delhi in the respective regions. Radio stations at the state capital or state level broadcast regional language bulletin.

AIR's national network broadcast 15-minute 'Morning News' and 'Samachar Prabhat' in English and Hindi respectively at 8.15 a.m. and 8.00 a.m. everyday. The Morning News includes a commentary and headlines in the day's newspapers in addition to the news. Also, there are hourly bulletins of five or ten minutes round-the-clock. Special bulletins are aired whenever necessary. It also broadcasts exclusive daily bulletins on sports, reports on the stock exchange. The News Service Division prepares all these bulletins.

(ii) Role of Newsreaders

Ans. A newsreader has an important role to play. A well-edited bulletin can be marred by bad news reading. At the same time, a poorly edited bulletin can be lifted up by a good newsreader. The older generation of listeners recall how in the past they remained tuned in to AIR just to listen to news reading by Melville de Mellow even when there may not have been much hard news in a bulletin. Attention must be paid to the speed of reading; it should not exceed 100 to 120 words a minute; Newsreaders can definitely be a guide to young listeners on correct pronunciation. A good voice, diction and pace of reading, giving pauses at the right points, make it worthwhile for anyone to tune in and listen to the news.

(iii) Challenge to Radio from Television

Ans. Today, radio is facing a big challenge from television and has been pushed into the background, especially in the metropolitan cities. In the developed world, say the US, Japan and Europe, where television is far more developed than in India, radio has made some adjustments in its programmes and found new areas for itself where it is doing well. In all these countries radio, news is still fastest means of communication. There is no reason why radio in India, including radio news, should not carve out a similar place for itself. Radio editors, reporters and newsreaders have to accept the challenge posed by television and give their listeners prompt, well-balanced and interesting news bulletins and news-related programmes. Radio needs to give latest local information to those who need it: housewives need to know about the market rates, and motorists about the state of roads. The weather conditions are as important for pilots or gliders or ham gliders and the like as for other citizens including agriculturists. The radio medium indeed has much potential.

Q5. Explain the all-important role of language in radio features and commentaries.

Ans. Voice, sound effects and music are the critical elements in the audio medium which gain the listeners attention and hold it. Thus, the voice of the commentator is crucial to a radio feature or a commentary. A commentator is both the eyes and ears of the listener. He creates verbal pictures in the minds of the receivers with his words. Background music and sound effects provide a creative fashion to the commentator's words.

Besides the language, the quality of voice, diction and intonation of the commentator matter most in a radio commentary. A radio commentator thus must make a deep study of a number of things before making the commentary. If it is about the funeral procession of a great leader, the tone has to match the mood and the feeling of the listeners. If it is a cricket match between India and Pakistan, the voice, diction and tone of the commentator must get in sync with the mood of the cricket fans. A commentator must have some basic knowledge about the subject he is commenting on.

The State of the Art: A commentator's job is not a cakewalk. He does lot of hard work to prepare an interesting and informative commentary. The road to success is an uphill task all the way. Ideally, a radio commentator would require a skillful combination of an observant eye, a ready tongue, nimble wit, imagination, tact and a sense of humour.

Commentary is an art and its successful practice depends on attention to a special technique-descriptive power and narrative style. This is possible only when one has the capacity to notice the finer details and also express them in simple but evocative terms. Without preliminary preparation, the commentators would find themselves in serious trouble. The best plans can be thrown out of gear by some unforeseen circumstance say a new twist to the event.

An intelligent and resourceful commentator will be able to place his thoughts and ideas across without much difficulty. In order to evoke a vivid word picture, one would require alert human faculties, and a vast knowledge of men and matters gathered through extensive reading and intensive involvement in the social, political and cultural developments in the country.

In short, a radio commentary describes an occasion or event in vivid words. The attempt is always to verify transport the distant listeners to the scene of action or attention. Naturally, the commentators has to be all ears and eyes to perform the job perfectly.

Step by Step Writing of Commentary/Feature: A commentator has to obtain all the information necessary about the location of the commentary broadcast: the occasion, the background information, technical terms and areas of emphasis. Accordingly, he will have to write the script or take notes. Usually, commentators visit the site of action, e.g., stadium, football or hockey ground, the scene of a cultural show, the route of a funeral ceremony, the cremation or burial ground, etc. This he does to familiarise himself with intricate, even trivial details and to trace the history leading up to the occasion, then he is ready to make a layout of the course as seen from one or more vantage points, and note all the important details,

Finally, before the broadcast day, he must keep a sharp lookout for any picturesque spots or amusing incidents to relate during the commentary.

Sometimes, technical snags can cause problems for the unprepared commentator. As a result of interrupted transmission the commentator may be forced to end the relay commentary at short notice.

Since the arrival of his plane was delayed by quite a few hours, the commentator had to go on and devise his own "show" to see him through his trouble. These days, one can promptly had the programme back to the studio in the face of any technical faults. Even that requires commentators with presence of mind to size up the situation without any panic.

Commenting is a balancing act: neither must he unnerve the listeners with monotonous, high-pitched or excited commentary from beginning to end nor must he slip up in what he says and thereby irk the listeners. Undoubtedly, rendering commentary is a job best left to mature people quick on the uptake, capable of talking any new development in their stride.

Word pictures created in the mind of the receiver drives the audio medium. A programme meant for broadcast such as a commentary, a feature or a play must not ignore the peculiarity. The effectiveness of a broadcast ultimately rests on the projection of one's personality through the microphone. Thus, broadcasting is not a mechanical process. "The technique of delivery is of fundamental importance", says late Prof. Harold Laski, to make a broadcast a success.

Q6. Enumerate the diverse skills required to prepare a commentary or narration for a feature on radio.

Or

Enumerate the various desirable attributes of the commentator and narrator.

Ans. To become a radio commentator/feature narrator, he must have certain essential physical characteristics. The word 'physical' implies the personality of the commentator as reflected in the credence and vibration of speech delivery which actually holds the key to success on the job. The various desirable attributes of the commentator and narrator are as follows:

(1) Broadcaster's Voice and Microphone Manners: Whether one is a commentator, interviewer, newsreader or announcer, one must take care of one's voice. To make a beginning, one needs to breathe correctly, enunciate clearly and attend to the vocal rhythm in order to ensure a liquid stream of pure sound. Breathing properly means breathing from the diaphragm as one does when asleep. This on turn helps us to speak rhythmically and the reserve breath helps to carry us smoothly from one sentence to another. Breathing from the diaphragm instead of the throat or through the nose also helps us to avoid extreme breathlessness, which the microphone is quick to catch and amplify. Hence, never speak on our last breath.

Proper enunciation is extremely important. This helps us to overcome the slurring of speech to a great extent. One way is to properly enunciate the consonants while leaving the vowels to look after themselves. How does one achieve this? By opening one's mouth widely to raise the soft palate and keeping the lower jaw forward. By doing so, we give free play to a remarkable variation of sound and the English language, in particular, is rich in sound. If one does not pay due attention to this aspect, one would throw away a wealth of meaning and emphasis.

(2) Speech Rhythm: Rhythm is the life blood of speech. Without this very important input, speech becomes lifeless and mechanical. Nothing kills a broadcast more surely than the monotony of delivery. Remember, words are the petrol of the speaker's thoughts, and rhythm is the oil that lubricates that vehicle. Therefore, the broadcaster's sound not only sends messages, but also ensures that the listener is persuaded by it. Again, every broadcast has to be kept alive and this is mainly achieved by correct emphasis, stress, and pause in the speech.

All top class commentators/broadcasters pitch their voices higher than used in ordinary speech. This is because the very low notes are apt to muffle the consonants, causing a booming effect on the microphone. Even so, in an interview, the lower the pitch of the broadcaster's voice, the less is the energy required. Also, there is less tendency to tighten the throat and back muscles. The low pitch is best for speech. However, it must be achieved with ease and not by suppressed sound. This definitely contributes to attractive and effective narration and commentary.

(3) Language: The broadcaster's language is indeed easy to understand because only the simplest possible terms are used. It is important to remember that the language be intelligible to the majority of the listeners. We must know that one picturesque phrase will do more to arouse the listener's interest than a bunch of literary and idiomatic expressions. Usually, a listener reacts quickly to the broadcaster's manner.

There are a few thumb rules which a broadcaster would do well to follow. We shall enumerate these rules here:

(i) Do not patronise the listeners.

(ii) Be friendly without being familiar.

(iii) Finally, we should be ourselves not what we would like the listeners to think we are.

(4) Avoid Padding: The term 'Padding' refers to the filling out of a sentence, publication, etc., with superfluous matter. A commentator must not pad out the narration. As a rule, avoid using unnecessary words, and admitting irrelevant contexts or distantly related topics in his scripts. One dull patch can imperil the broadcaster's hold on the listeners. A commentator should never let his script or commentary/narration meander even for a moment.

Q7. Write various tips to write a good script for radio.

Ans. Right mix of words and sounds makes an effective script for a radio commentary. Some important tips for a good script are as follows:

- **Keep the Script/Commentary Moving:** Use shorter sentences that make narration crisper. Avoid padding at all costs. Briefly explain all the points towards the end of the narration. Reception of the main points is necessary to ensure that we have told him them about all the points that we want our listeners to remember.
- **Enliven the Script/Commentary:** Enliven the script with intelligent use of vocabulary. The wider the use of vocabulary, the more visual are our images. It helps us to vary our form and have a firm hold over listeners/audience.
- **Be Completely Natural:** Be natural while giving commentary as though we were talking. If it sounds like formal written language. We will immediately know we are off-the-track. Ask to friends and well-wishers to help with their reactions. This will be immense help in improving performance.
- **Keep Cliches Out:** Do not use cliches. It will make script difficult to understand. Explain if there is any use will cliches in the script.
- **Keep on Looking for the Needs of the Market:** Know the target audience and their taste. Accordingly use the words. Script should be simple and conjure visual rather than oral

images is the listeners mind. Short sentences and short words are always more effective than long-winded and pedantic phrases.

- **Do not Talk Down to the Audience:** Do not sound like to know everything and teacher is talking down to the students. Be professional to explain some matter. In a running commentary, must take precaution against any slip of the tongue that would offend a listener.

Q8. Explain in all-important role of language in radio features and commentaries.

Ans. The language of speech (the spoken word) differs considerably from the language of writing (the written word). The differences arise in the:

- Vocabulary,
- Sentence length,
- Sentence structure,
- Density of distribution of information, the
- Writer speaker's intention and attitude to the subject and toward the listeners.

The important factors which make or mar a commentary are the

- Stress on syllabus and the
- Accent of one's speech together
- Amount of information and
- Actual speed of delivery.

One must take into account the varying spans of memory and levels of comprehension of different listeners. Clarity of both content and actual narration is thus essential.

One must remember that it is an individual's memory and comprehension that we deal with. Listeners generally cannot turn to anybody for explanation. All the necessary aids to memory and comprehension are, generally built into the programme material. Scripts for radio commentary and features ought to be written with this vital factor in view. The narrators too must be chosen with due care given instructions about the required pace of narration, style of delivery, etc.

The radio is an audio medium. The secret of the ideal radio broadcast is the unexpressed will to woo listeners to stay tuned for the entire programme by simply providing the right fare. A good radio feature or running commentary is one that strives to describe the subject or phenomenon cogently and comprehensively. A radio feature and commentary is written in words that create appropriate atmosphere and concrete pictures in the listener's mind. It is by improving the script and presenting it creatively that a radio feature writer and commentator make even the most complex subject appear simple. It is in their hands to make the listening a gainful and lasting pleasure. They have only to wield their power correctly to endear themselves to their audience.

Q9. Define Television News. Discuss about print and broadcast news.

Ans. Newscast is a regularly scheduled television program that reports current events. News is typically reported in a series of individual stories that are presented by one or more anchors.

News may be any item of importance that takes place in a certain locality, something unusual, something that interest us, or concerns us. The classic definition of news known to all beginners is not really a definition but an illustration.

- While the news is fundamentally the same in any medium–newspapers, radio or television–yet the presentation of news differs in all the three media owing to special characteristics.
- Stories for the broadcast media generally are shorter than those for the print.
- Time is to radio/television what space is to a newspaper.
- The newspaper's space is expandable, but broadcast time is not.
- The length of a news broadcast severely restricts the number of news items that can be incorporated into the broadcast bulletin.
- Time limitations force broadcast persons to be highly selective in the stories meant for inclusion in news bulletins. That is why news for broadcast media is covered with extreme brevity as compared with the newspaper coverage.
- The broadcast stories must be concise and intelligible because the listener/viewer has only one chance to grasp the meaning. He or she cannot go back to the story the way a newspaper reader can. Therefore, stories written for broadcast must be

conversational and easy to comprehend. Good broadcast copy must be easy on the ears.

- The old newspaper rule of including five Ws and one H in the first paragraph of a story does not necessarily apply to broadcast news. To write clear news copy for broadcast we must remember to determine what is important in the story. Does the story lie in what happened? Or is it who it happened to? Or, perhaps how it happened? Or, it is what is happening or who will become involved? These questions must be answered in our mind before we can write a broadcast news story.

When writing for television, the pauses necessary to coordinate words with visuals are taken into consideration. Writing is often geared to the available pictures of the event. The words omit what the pictures show and tell what the pictures omit. Because of the visual element, the TV news-show tends to favour news stories which can be reported with pictures to news on which no picture is available.

Q10. What are the basic rules that must be remembered in writing the news for television?

Ans. Television news is different from print and radio news, especially because of the visuals. TV news writing is also different from news for newspapers and magazines. News for TV are generally shorter than compared to stories on newspapers because of time constraints.

The basic rules to write for a television news are as follows:

(1) Clarity: The TV news story should be clear at once. The visuals given should be in sync with the stories and must be placed at the appropriate position.

(2) Brevity: The sentences in TV news should be short and simple. Long sentences are difficult to understand. A sentence should have 13 to 14 words. Short syllabic words are always better in television news. If we have one syllabic word always use that word instead of two or three syllabic words. Excess syllables represent waste. A one-syllable word is always better than a two-syllable word, if it says what we want to say. And a two-syllable word is much better than a four-syllable word when it serves the purpose. Often we can save time by using:

"Try" for "attempt"

"Urge" for "persuade"

"End" for "conclude"

"First" for "initial"
"Beat" for "defeat"
"Buy" for "purchase"
"Sure" for "certain"

One syllable words are often either familiar verbs, pronouns, function words (the "glue" words which hold content words together), or concrete nouns. Long words such as capitalism, totalitarianism, communication, psychotherapy often communicate abstract ideas. In writing news for TV, we cannot always escape long words. To get a difficult idea across, we should do it in as simple a manner as possible.

(3) Conversational: TV news writers should use everyday words, the language of conversation. TV journalists use a vocabulary that corresponds to the one used in daily conversation. Words used in everyday speech ought to be included when drafting news for television. Consider the following example:

Newspaper style: "The vice-president of the New Delhi branch of the Red Cross stated in a press conference on Tuesday that many toys can inflict injury upon unsuspecting youngsters". This is not exactly conversational. Instead, a TV journalist should write: "A Red Cross official warns that many toys can be dangerous for children". Given below are few examples of words which are generally too formal for TV news, with conversational alternatives:

Formal	**Conversational**
Passed away	died
Residence	home
Prior to	before
Indisposed	sick, ill

(4) Time Reference-Present Tense: TV news should have the element of immediacy. Reporters should must try to make the report up-to-date and present the copy in such a manner that the news should sound fresh and timely. To achieve this goal, the news should be written in present tense. The present tense is the most engaging in the language. It shows that the action is still going on and conveys currency of the news.

It is more appropriate to phrase a sentence as, "There is huge fire in the market", than, "there was a huge fire in the market". Similarly, use "Iraq announces that it accepts the UN proposal for a cease fire in West Asia" instead of "Iraq announced that it accepted the UN proposal for a cease fire in West Asia".

However, actions that belong to moments in the recent past cannot be forcibly dragged into the present-that bridge is not collapsing now.

However, (the present perfect tense) maintains an air of immediacy while describing actions that have ended.

A building has collapsed /A building collapses

A man has been shot/A man is being shot (both are acceptable)

The present perfect should be used in situations in which the present tense is unacceptable. The present perfect is less dated than the past tense.

For Example: Use "A man has been arrested for impersonating as a magistrate" instead of "A man had been arrested for impersonating as a magistrate".

In some situations, neither the present nor the present perfect tense is acceptable. It is unacceptable to say "

(i) Few people have shown up at the meeting, so it broke up. Early" and

(ii) Two people have been shot earlier today". In such cases, the past tense should be used. So the sentences should be"

(iii) Few people showed up at the meeting, so it broke up early" and "Two people were shot earlier today".

TV news reporters should always provide the latest information. If the news has broken yesterday, do not say "today". Such a practice can prove embarrassing. If it is mid-afternoon and we are reporting an incident that occurred the previous night, do not use the time. For example, if we are using a statement that the Prime Minister made the preceding night, it is not necessary to say:

Last night Prime Minister Manmohan Singh issued a strong statement condemning terrorist violence in Punjab and Kashmir. Instead, we can say "Prime Minister Manmohan Singh has condemned terrorist violence in Punjab and Kashmir." The time element can be mentioned later in the story when details are mentioned.

Active Voice: In TV news writing, avoid the use of passive voice. Instead use the active voice where the subject acts upon the object. It is better to say, "The fire destroyed the building" instead of saying "The building was destroyed by the fire."

Q11. Write some basic news scripts of television.

Ans. Television news presentation is governed by script writing. Written for the spoken word, it is written to be heard or for the ear. Script must be written so that the audience understands it the first time it is heard. The pictures accompanying the script should make it easier to understand what is said. TV news should have some extra qualities to give it a distinct flavour to suit the medium. Some of the qualities are discussed below:

- **Talking Heads:** TV news story without visuals is called talking heads. This skeletal news story is also called a "reader", or "liner". A newscaster reads the news with no visual appearing on the screen. Story without visuals find its way into the TV news bulletin because there are occasions when no visuals are available especially on out-of-town stories, or in the case of a story that broke late, taking it impossible to get relevant footage on the air. Also, some particularly complex stories may be better understood without the added distraction of visuals.
- **Super:** Bits of information superimposed on the TV screen are called supers. Also called IDS, 'supers' are also important elements to every story with video in it. They identify or explain a person, thing, place or picture. For example, they are used to identify the newscasters by supering their names on their images.
- **Voice-over (VO):** A talking head along with a visual is called voice over. A visual can be photograph, chart, map or graph. It is used to illustrate a story, identify a place, or simplify a complex economic news item say with the use of graph. The voice-over or the narration continues over the visuals. Besides static visuals like graphics, illustrations, etc. the voiceover is also carried on video footage of for example, a plane crash on a mountain summit, or riot-hit areas. Shortly after the newscaster begins a story on camera, video coverage appears on the screen while the newscaster continues to read.
- **Sound-bite:** In a sound-bite, the newscaster begins on camera and reads up to certain point in the script; then the expert interviewed on the subject appears on videotape, making a comment related to the story. The anchor-person reappears at the end of the sound bite, so as to tag the story before moving on to another news item.

- **Stand-up:** Like the sound bite, stand-up is a story assembled by a staff reporter. The newscaster begins on-camera and reads up to a certain point and then introduces the reporter. The latter then speaks from the location. These types of stories are the backbone of newscast. Reporters read the stand-up while looking straight into the camera.
- **Package:** Sound-bite plus stand-up is called package. The treatment for package is the same as in the case of stand-up except that the story may include an interview with an expert eyewitness apart from the reporter's footage. The newscaster begins a news item with a brief mention of the highlights of the story and follows it up by introduce the reporter on location. The reporter then states the main points of the news and gives details in a concise style, the report may be interspersed with interviews of the persons in the news. These comments not only fill the gaps in the report but also lend an air of credibility to the reporter's inferences.

Q12. List all the possible sources of news for a TV Station.

Ans. There are many source, basis, supplier, informant, spokesperson and origins of a television news story. News sources are the ways and means through which a TV channel gets news. Television newsrooms generally use the same sources of news that are used by the other media. However, of late, two main sources of news for Doordarshan have come to be booked: The satellite/microwave video feed services and syndicated video coverage.

- The primary sources of news on television are the news wire services such as Press Trust of India (PTI) and United News of India (UNI) among other news agencies. Still photographs transmitted by facsimile wire services are also used on television, especially those of late-breaking stories for which moving pictures are not available.
- The satellite/microwave video feed is television's own unique version of wire service. It is an electronic transmission of news stories originally recorded on film or video and sent by closed circuit microwave or through satellite to subscribers who record it on their own video tape and then decide which stories to use for inclusion in their own local TV news-shows.

- The biggest source of news for any station is its reporting staff. The reporters live in the community to which they are telecasting through everyday contact with people in the area, from their observations as they move in the society and from their informers they get news for their organization. Therefore, the chief assignment of the reporter is to get news for the channel he or she is attached with. Most stations employ correspondents/reporters who gather news by going out with a camera crew to report an incident event such as a fire, an accident, a conference, etc. At times, owing to the absence of a visual, the reporter may file a dry story (a story without any visual) or instead speak to the camera and narrate the story.
- Film/video coverage of many spot news events such as accidents, fires, floods, earthquake, and the like is often difficult to procure if staff correspondents/camera person are not available at the time of event. However, such an event is sometimes covered by a freelance camera person scouting around near the scene. This visual coverage is purchased from the freelance camera-persons who are known as stringers. The stations have to rely on stringers for unexpected news stories, particularly if the staff cameraperson is unable to reach the scene fast enough to record it.
- Most television stations monitor radio news bulletins and vice versa for important news stories. If the story is very significant and there is not time to obtain visuals, such stories are telecast dry.

Q13. Enumerate various basic style rules of Television.

Ans. Attempts at some kind of standardization do, of course, take place from time to time, with varying degrees of success. Editors looking for continuity will occasionally assign senior journalists to produce lists of preferred spellings, titles and phrases to match the standards of ethical behaviour they expect from their staff.

Every television station generally has its own rules of news writing. TV news writing also depends on the abilities of the reporters and correspondents and the expertise of the camera men. However, there are some basic rules of TV news writing. Some of the rules are as follows:

(1) Typing: All news items to be telecast must be type-written in triple space. If it is for radio, use the full page allowing about an inch for margins. For television, use the right half (or two-thirds) of page for news copy. Keep the left side of the page for video information-visual effects, film or video tape rolls. Type the news in all caps or upper-lower case.

Write the date on the first page of your script. Write your initials of last name in the upper left hand corner of every page. Use paragraphs for easy reading. Number the stories. For a news item, if you need more than one page is required, complete the sentence if every page and if possible do not continue the paragraph to the next page.

(2) Corrections: When we are making correction, cross the word sentence we want to delete or black it out completely. Do not leave anything ambiguous in the script. A news reader has read the copy and everything should be clear.

(3) Numbers: Always simplify complicated numbers. Do not give fractions or decimals in the copy. For convenience, use terms like "approximately", "more than", "about" and "almost". For instance, ₹1,001,897.46 in most cases should be written as "slightly more than ten lakh rupees".

Spell out all numbers up to eleven. Spell out fractions and decimal points as three-fourths, one-half, three point two.

(4) Quotations: In TV news, there should be fewer quotes compared to newspaper stories because there is no time for extended quotations. News on TV/radio is short and very precise as compared to newspaper reporters.

(5) Abbreviations: Try not to use of abbreviations in broadcast news writing. Common sense should be exercised when handling names of government agencies or phrases that are sometimes conveniently written as acronyms. Most familiar abbreviations and acronyms such as the USA or CBI can be used. If it is "Lieutenant-Governor", write it out in full and out "Lt.-Gov".

(6) Attribution: Do not follow the newspaper structure in attributing a quote. This is referred to as "dangling attribution". Do not write, "I am going to win the election", says Mr. D.N. Rao. For two reasons, in TV news does not use such attributions: (i) People do not talk that way, and (ii) The listener may think that the words are those of the broadcaster. Instead it should be written as Mr. D.N. Rao said he would win the election. Or in these exact words, Mr. D.N. Rao said, "I am going to win the election".

Q14. What are the techniques of television news reporting? Discuss some basic and essential qualification of a television news reporter.

Ans. The TV news reporter is the eyes, ears, and legs of TV newsroom. The reporter must get the "facts" on each story assigned to him/her. And sometimes, particularly in small TV news operations, he/she should also be able to shoot news film besides reporting the story. The specific duties of a staff reporter include:

- gathering and reporting local and area-specific news and features;
- writing and editing news;
- presenting news on the air, conducting interviews, AD LIB reports, etc., either in the studio or from location.

Qualifications of TV News Reporter: To perform well on the job, a television news reporter has to possess some basic and essential qualifications. Some of these are given below:

- Versatility;
- Good writing skills;
- A liberal education;
- Excellent understanding of the TV medium;
- Integrity;
- Photogenic face/pleasing personality;
- Good voice-quality;
- Confidence.

The best television videotape of film can almost be shown silent. The pictures themselves tell the story. When covering a story for television, reporters have to make sure that as much of the meaning of the story gets into the camera as is possible. To be able to comprehensively cover the news, television news reporters generally employ the following techniques.

(1) Piece to Camera: Of all the skills needed for television news reporting, the piece to camera is amongst the most frequently used. The piece to camera, which is essentially in-vision, is recorded on location. It has three advantages: it immediately establishes the reporter's presence on the spot; it is extremely simple to execute, and it is fast enough to be considered a kind of contingency sample.

These stand-ups are written on the scene, without the benefit of typewriters or the other conveniences of the newsroom. Since the reporter looks straight into the camera, the lines have to be memorized. Sometimes, the reporters read from a note-book or a clip-board after ensuring the opening paragraph, at least, is word perfect.

Most stand-ups are short–10 to 20 seconds. On some occasions, they run longer especially in complex stories that require a lot explaining, but do not offer many visuals. A stand-up can also be used in the middle of a story to "bridge" two other sections of the report. Bridges work especially well when the reporter demonstrates something.

(2) Studio Spots: While the piece to camera is an in-vision news presentation by the reporter recorded on location, the studio spot is a news item read in the studio someone other than the programme's main presenter, as additional information to the visuals. Usually, it is a special correspondent or a reporter who is called upon to draw together the elements of a news story with or without the aid of videotape or illustration.

Because television news is a team effort involving many persons, the chances of human error are great in a studio set-up, particularly in an 'on-air' situation. There are four simple rules that the on-camera studio reporter/correspondent should follow:

- Maintain self-control. Expect problems and be prepared cope with them;
- Always prepare file copy. If film or video tape fails to come up, have the file copy close at hand, to carry on the show;
- Never pick nose or scratch; and
- Be familiar with studio cue-signals.

Q15. Write a short note on "Writing to Visuals."

Ans. Visuals are no doubt very important in a TV news, but in many instances the narration behind the film is responsible for the success of visual news stories on television. The effectiveness of visuals can be affected by poorly written narration.

Following are the three basic rules which a TV reporter must follow while writing to visuals:

- Do not give full details in the narration;

- The narration and visuals must go together. The words must relate to the pictures;
- When the film rolls on, tell the story or describe it as it happened. Of course, we may begin with a brief opening summary.

Writing narration is one of the most skills in broadcast reporting. The language should also crisp, the timing should be exact and the words have to click with the visuals.

Q16. What is the art of television interviews? Explain the guidelines for it.

Ans. A television newspaper must be a good interviewer to become a good reporter whether talking face to face with a political personality or an expert, or may be when asking questions in front of a television camera, the newsperson must know how to conduct an interview. Prepare the questions in advance, These should be short and to the point.

During the interview allow the subject talk. It is his/her opinions, ideas and thoughts that are important. If subject's answers are not clear, or if they are insufficient, pursue the question further. Use the direct approach if subject is hostile. Do not turn a conversation into a battle by being aggressive.

Guidelines for Interviewers:

- There is much difference between interviews without camera and light and interviews with light and camera. In a TV interview, whether it is on-line recording or recorded on videotape for later broadcast, a reporter has to think quickly to follow up with topics outside the originally planned structure of the interview. He should have the ability to marshal and arrange thoughts so that he can ask questions logically.
- Besides, the questions should be properly phrased. Reporters should not make long statements while asking questions. This irritates the viewers who are interested to the views of subject.
- Avoid the cliches like, "Now, what do you feel about.......?" or "What about the future..........?"

  Such questions stimulate the interviewee into saying nothing more interesting than a few adjectives. Ask questions to get something interesting from the interviewee.

- Avoid direct question which can be replied with either "yes" or "no". Start a question with any of the Ws (Who, What, When, Where, Which and Why) or How.
- Questions which are too general should be avoided like "Has your father's death changed your views on the meaning of life?" or "Do you think the police will catch the culprits?"

Research for TV Interviews: Research is crucial to get information for a TV programme, including interviews. Through research we can look for

- guests as interviewees
- facts, opinions and ideas,
- visual materials, films and slides
- graphics, photographs, drawing, maps and other visuals.

Warming up for the Interview: We speak very comfortably with a "warm audience", with family and friends who laugh at our jokes and sympathize with our requirements. But in the face of a large or critical audience, we become choosy in picking words and our performance drops. The perfect interviewer thus would evince keen interest in the subject and make the guest forget the audience watching him through the TV camera.

During an interview, the difficult task for the reporter is to listen to your the instead of reading the prepared question. Listening to the guest encourages him to shed any inhibitions and reply freely to his/her questions. The reporter can pick up the thread of thought and follow naturally with the next question.

Question for TV Interviews: A TV interview should be like a conversation and not a cross-examination. To achieve this, the interviewer has to remain alert and watch when and how a person responds to non-verbal reactions, say commands, reactions, comments and even gestures of hand and face like lifting your eyebrows or frowning.

The following are some types of reaction to what subject says, reporter can make the audience sit up and take note:

- Expressing surprise or wonder at appropriate time. Such reaction of the reporter/interviewer draws the audience's reaction to the importance of what the guest has said. It also makes the interviewee reacts and comment.

- Mild disbelief with words such as "Not really" with slight overtones of kidding compels the guest to confirm some action and defend it with emphasis.
- Showing empathy by saying like "That must have been .... You must have been delighted", encourages the interviewee to speak openly.
- Drop expressions lie "I see" or "Un-hun". These sound very awkward and this is the beginner's way of filling time until an appropriate question comes to mind.
- Listen attentively, take interest and show it Laugh at jokes your interviewee cracks.
- If there is any obscure point, intervene and make it clear to the audience.
- In between the replies of the interviewee and reporter's question, add information and seek comments on the same.
- Tell the background of the interviewee to the viewers. It at the beginning. Inform these why guest's opinion or comments are worth listening to.
- Use the information found from research. Ask him like "Once you said ....". Such questions will compel your guest's to comment on that or he might say something new or add to what he had said earlier.
- Ask question like
  "What happened then?"
  "What did you see there?"
  "What did you do then?"
  "What did you do that?"
  "What did you notice after that?"
  "What did he say".

Q17. Define television script. Explain the preparation for scripting.

Ans. A full television script for a recorded item or programme will have a great deal of information of relevance to many different people. As a result there is no uniform format.

A TV script differs from a radio script is that it has a visual component in addition to the audio content. Evidently, music and video is prominent out although undoubtedly the narration, dialogue, music and sound effects contribute to the overall effect of the programme. Yet the audio and video content require careful blending to make a compact whole right from the script stage. The two should match each other and never be antagonistic. The audio, i.e. the sound content of the TV programme, ought to contribute to the video, i.e. the visual content of the TV programme, by adding a distinct flavour of its own. The final programme has to be visualized fully on paper first. Only they can the later stages of 'production' and 'post-production' of a programme be planned and carried out successfully.

Preparation for scripting–the Recce: Initial research for writing a script can be conducted among books and other print material, on interest and by talking to people over telephone or face to face. In the second stage, we must visit various locations and sites to see and experience the subject first. We have to get some kind of feel for the place, its sounds, smell and general atmosphere. For this job, the writer himself should visit since the actually of places changes all kinds of previously held ideas and misconceptions.

Recce before Writing: The main objective of a recce is to enable the writer to fill the skeleton of the outline with the flesh of practical scenes which can be recorded in picture and sound.

During the recce, the writer has to absorb impressions, note scenes and character and their saying. At this time, all should be tentative and the writer should not make any firm commitments to possible participants. After he collected all the information, he should return to the base. After that he should give himself a day or two to forget the chaff and inessentials, he will be in a position to give a shape and order the material into the most telling and effective script. The writer should not refer to his notes until the broad sweep of the script has been committed on paper. After that he should check the accuracy of his recollection.

After the recce, the writer has to fit all the additional information in the outline. While fitting in the formation, the writer has to adhere to the outline if the structure and clarity of the programme is to be preserved.

All manner of interesting sidelights revealed by the recce have to be excluded if they cannot be contained within the chosen central theme and its development. The central theme, its statement development and final resolution should run like backbone through the programme. Remember that no programme can cope with more than one theme.

Q18. Differentiate between the following:

(i) TV Script Vs. Newspaper Article

Ans. Script of any program is written in a very different way for the two areas of communication. Scripting a topic for a TV programme differs significantly from writing a piece about the same subject for the newspapers. In the former the words are not too literary, rather they are colloquial and revolve around the terms used in every day speech. The audio content of the script has to facilitate easy registration on the viewers even as they absorb all the visual information. The audio must neither be long-winding nor detract from the overall effect of the video. It must be clear in one go. On television, it is not possible to recheck and go back to the information once again. However, this is now partially possible with the Teletext information on 'pages'. Each of these pages remains on the screen for a given duration, to enable the viewers to read the information on screen. In any other TV programme, returning to the words once they are uttered is not possible. Whereas in a newspaper, the reader can go back and forth at will and 'recall' the information when required.

(ii) TV Script Vs. Radio Script

Ans. Radio is an aural medium which involves only hearing sense of people where as TV has both audio and visual impacts on mind. It is necessary for a radio program to create a mind picture for listeners and to convey the message in the right direction. There are the key differences between radio script and television script:

- **Scenes and Sequences:** Radio plays are divided into sequences. Every sequence should end with a fade or a cut. The passage of time may be indicated by music or a silence leaving no doubt in the mind of listeners as where and when the action is taking place. Whereas TV play is divided in scenes and every scene appeared with establishing shot. Every scene is on the screen.
- **Characterization:** An essential element in a radio play. Limit the number of characters to maximum four at a time. And the story should revolve around single person. Beware of characters that are very much a like to avoid the confusion for the listeners, such as mothers of two friends. Unless there is some obvious difference in terms of temperament or accent.

Whereas, in TV play there is not such limitation of characters. Story may revolve around more than 8 or 9 people it will not be difficult for the viewers to remember the character as every character is on screen.

- **Dialogue:** Dialogue writing is another important element of radio plays as it involves verbal communication so it must be expressive as much as possible. The delivery of words creates a mind picture so that the play must be written by keeping the visual sense. An attracting opening is necessary which can grab the attention of listeners. Avoid using such words which cause tongue twist and the unnecessary dialogues should also be avoided. Every dialogue must make its contribution for the story as a whole and move the plot onward. Where as in TV play viewers can see movements of characters the face expressions, body language as far it is concerned. It embraces the non-verbal communication as well. For example, a tragic scene can be shown only through tears on TV but on radio emotions should be shown through words.
- **Stress and Pause:** In radio plays, it is very necessary to mention the stress and pause in a dialogue. Because the meanings can be changed through a wrong stress and pause in speech. For example, there is a sentence "I did not say that you are a liar" which can be delivered through 4 different ways. Where as in TV plays it is not as much necessary because the audience can judge the situation through visuals.
- **Creativity:** In radio plays, sound effects and actualities bring expressions to the script. Such as sound of applause, cheers, clapping, opening of door, pouring water in glass or sound of boots etc. it may also include sound of waves, blowing of winds, rainfall or thunderstorm. These all make a script alive. Where as in TV plays creativity is the art of camera shots. More over TV play can be made artistic through special lights, video graphics, wardrobe, set design, make up, jewelry and props etc.
- **Visual Sense:** In radio plays, the script must be written to keep in view the visual sense. Such as movements should be written in words for example, "Nadia – you are doing ninety! Slow down the car" (which means Nadia is going at the speed of 90

km per hr) where as TV carry both audio and visual sense for the audience. Any weakness of script can be overcome through visuals. Although script must be powerful but there is no need to tell the movements in words.

Q19. Describe the process of developing a TV script.

Ans. It is time consuming the methodical process of developing a script. Nevertheless, it plays dividends to follow a stepwise procedure:

- To conceptualise or concept formation is the first step.
- Then the writing of the treatment of this proposal.
- Third, preparing the drafts of scripts after filling in information in the treatment after recce.
- Fourth, finalising the script for shooting.

(1) Concept: Concept formation is the threading together of a concept or theme through the programme. After the initial research on the topic is conducted, the TV programme producer writes out a proposal or enlists the services of a scriptwriter to create the structure of the script or he may engage a scriptwriter from the beginning to conceptualise the programme, write the treatment for the topic and a detailed script.

(2) Treatment and Master Scene: The Treatment is an outline of the content-both audio and video - of a proposed programme. On its basis, a writer pens the script for a programme. The Treatment will have an outline of likely camera shots, important scenes and situation. It works as a reference when the script is being developed and finalised.

Before writing the Treatment, an extensive research has to be carried out. On every aspect of the proposed programme-including the locations, costumes and content. Research conducted in these and other related aspects enhance the quality of the programme. The content will be factual if it is a documentary. Fictional content is permitted in documentary drama. Documentary can be categorised on the basis of its subject whether social, sports, environmental, personality portrait and legal etc. The Master Scene Treatment is a broad description of the visuals and action along with the possible dialogues and narration. It comes in between the Treatment and the shooting script. It looks like the text of a play. It carries rather more exact descriptions of the scenery and explicit stage directions. If the project has to be approved by the non-TV people like sponsors, vetting government departments and financiers, it is easier for them to comprehend the Master Scene Treatment than the more detailed shooting script.

(3) Draft Scripts: The TV script has two different components - the visuals and the audio. The break-up of the visuals has to be written on the left hand side of the page and the corresponding audio is mentioned on the right hand. In draft scripts, many additions and deletions are made the script is finalised.

Shooting Script or Camera Script: In the shooting script, the camera shots are specified along with various scenes and sequences. It details the shotwise script and guides the shooting. In a film, there will be different types of shots based on the content, size of subject and angle from which the subject is shown. Given below are different types of shot:

- **Long shot (LS):** It is a shot that shows the subject from a distance.
- **Close-up:** It is a shot where the main subject occupies most or all of the picture frames.
- **Medium shot or mid shot (MS):** In this shot, the subject is shot at normal viewing distance, and cuts actors usually at the waistline.
- **High angle shot:** In this shot, the subject is taken from above.
- **Low angle shot:** In this shot, the subject is taken from below.
- **Singleton:** A shot that shows one person or thing.
- **Two shot:** A shot that shows two persons.
- **Over the shoulder shot (OS):** A shot taken with the camera positioned behind one of the subjects.

Every shot has a specific impact on the subject. For example, a low angle shot makes a person (the subject) appears powerful and frightening. A high angle shot of a person makes the person appear small and weak.

Shooting Script: Given below is an example of a shooting script.

Day I

(1) Dining room: Sun light coming through window. Mrs. Sinha (reaching for a spoon and looking at her husband) What is the issue that people in the colony were discussing about?

Two-shot: Mr. Sinha and Mrs. Seated at dining table.

(2) MCS: Mr. Sinha buried behind a newspaper.

Mr. Sinha.

(distractedly) Mmmmm?

(3) CU: Mrs. Sinha at table, taking rice on a plate Mrs. Sinha (PETULANTLY)

Will you take your nose out of that paper and talk to me.

(4) (Over the shoulder) Two shot favouring: Mr. Sinha still behind his paper, Mrs. Sinha glaring at him (SHOT over Mrs. Sinha's shoulder, looking towards Mr. Sinha).

For reference in production and editing, it is useful to number each shot. Also, label it INT for interior, EXT for exterior, "Day" to indicate to daytime and NIGHT for night time.

If there is any camera movement, mention it in the script for the camera person's reference. Write "Pan" for a movement of the camera with respect to its vertical axis. Horizontal pan right is the movement of the camera from its static position to its right. Pan left refers to the camera movement from its static position toward the left. Tilt refers to the camera movement vertically. Tilt up or tilt down are the instructions to move the camera up or down vertical plane.

The Need for Multiplicity of Camera Positions: We need to take so many shots sometimes because at the precise moment the viewers want it and require additional information.

For example, someone is shooting a man sawing a plank. First one is an opening long shot of the man. Just as the viewers are wondering about the identity of the person in the back garden, the scene cuts to show a medium shot of the man approaching a plank. Just as the viewers wonder what the man is doing, they see the medium close shot of the man beginning to saw. Now the viewer wonders what is he sawing? The close-up of shot 4 clearly shows the plank. Is sawing difficult the viewer wonders. So, the close-up of the man's face in shot 5 shows is look of concentration. Each new shot appears precisely at the moment when the viewers subconsciously demand the next piece of information. If the timing of the subsequent editing is right, the viewers will not even to aware of the separate shots. The viewers will be provided the shot they want as and when they want it.

Editing Script: On the basis of footage obtained after shooting the programme, the editing script is written. In the editing script, the transitions from one shot to the next are mentioned along with the duration of every shot. The cassette number containing the shot and the counter reading of the cassette at that particular shot is also mentioned.

- The transition from one shot to the next may be a Cut, Dissolve, Wipe.
- In Dissolve, there will be a progressive superimposition of a picture on another until the second picture replaces the first.
- In Wipe, one picture slides across the screen, wiping out another.

Q20. How do we present a TV commentary? Discuss.

Ans. Commentary leads addresses the traditional who, what and when. If this information had been reported on TV or radio the day before, this lead might not be a good one for the print edition of the newspaper; however, if the reporter had an exclusive or posted this information online as soon as it became available, then this lead would make sense. In an outdoor event telecast or in a pre-recorded film, a TV commentary is required. As it is delivered out of vision (DDV), the voice quality and the commentary itself take on added importance.

Scripting a TV Commentary: The commentary and video should merge as one whole. The visuals may be self-explanatory or require commentary to accompany them. The commentary must fit the video with great precision. It is for this reason that the commentary must be well-scripted. Of course, the quality of the commentary can make or mar the video. The words used to depict ideas and thoughts and perceptions must be apt, clear and contain a natural flow of their own.

Presenting a TV Commentary: In a commentary, the speaker's voice, tone, speed, accent, stress on the right syllables, pauses at the correct junctures, all assume importance. When the face, gesture and other non-verbal expressions are not in view, the voice, its quality and manner of expression take on an added significance. The commentator must also match the visuals on the screen and explain the context of the action being shown. The timing of the commentary should be precise and coincide with the pictures. This is especially the case in a pre-recorded programme. In a running commentary for a direct telecast of an outdoor event, firstly, the event is news worthy and as a consequence, its video coverage is extremely important. Secondly, a lot of preparation goes into 'scripting' the commentary. Research and collection of interesting aspects about the event and its precedents ought to be carried out and all information double-checked, as this would be a basis to deliver the commentary. It is best to leave the running commentary unscripted, while at the same time referring to the information we have accumulated for the purpose of our 'script'. In other words, we write down the information that we collect in the course of our research and memorize most of it, keeping our papers at hand for ready reference. Even so, as we speak our commentary, so sure must we be of the information and its context that we need not read the notes we have made, but instead reel off the points coherently and with ease. Our viewers will then be able to comprehend what we say.

It is an art to recognise the patches when commentary is not necessary. If the picture says, it all there is no need to add to it. The purpose of a commentary is to identify and make clear the content and context of the images on the screen. The commentary has to complement the visual information, fulfill the curiosity of the viewer about any item in the picture frame and may also include anecdotes and interesting piece of information.

The commentator must constantly remind himself that talking down to the viewer is best avoided. It is no singular virtue to be speaking into the microphone to an audience. On the other hand, it would definitely pay dividends to be adopting a stance of sharing ones knowledge and perceptions with the viewers.

❑❑❑

5 EDITING

INTRODUCTION

In a news organisation, editing plays a pivotal role. A news item or a news story, as it is called, is written by hurried reporters and is rough-edged like raw diamond. Hence, the copy is polished and honed by a team of editors, who form the Editorial Desk. The team is also called the desk persons, works under tremendous pressure and severe time constraint. By editing, we mean preparing a news report for publication, telecast or broadcast. Editing is a process by which are port is read, corrected, modified, value-added, polished, improved and made better for publication. Condensation is also part of editing. The editor also decides whether photographs or other images or graphs should be used along with the report. It requires skills, art and a lot attention. It is equally important as the news item. Having considered the editing skills and artwork involved in the news items and photographs. A good editor needs creative skills, command over the language, ideas to improve the copy and correct judgement about how much importance should be given for a particular news item. Speedy transmission of news is as important as the actual news gathering. It has been made possible by the advanced electronic equipment. Electronic editing means editing on screen with a software program that can track the editing changes and provide an edit trail for review.

Q1. Discuss the concept of Editing for news.

Ans. The word edit is synonymous to prepare, correct, tidy up, check over, revise, amend, change, alter, modify, adjust, transform and this all is done while editing any written item as well as the news.

Editing is an art and a technique, which involves a number of activities: revising, amending, checking, correcting, polishing, rephrasing, rewriting. It also means putting together, rearranging, reordering and selecting the material to be finally published.

Editing may also be defined as correcting and adapting the text of an article, news story or a book that make it suitable for publishing: Collecting several pieces of writing by different authors and preparing them for publishing. It is the work of a team of skilled persons those while working in a newspaper, can scan the vast see of words, make a selection, cut down what is selected to size and serve it up attractively to its readers. There has to be selection because, irrespective of the size of the paper, the amount of material that a newspaper gets is much more than it has the space to print.

All incoming news items, collectively called copy, is sifted, before being processed, to achieve a balance of news between that originating within the organisation and that pouring in from outside. Only the newsworthy stories are finally selected. These are checked for grammar, syntax, facts, figures and also clarified for betterment and are condensed for economy of space.

The news copy is written by experienced and inexperienced people, and, hence, lack uniformity. The copy has different shapes, follow a different style, and generally lack readability. The news reporters are the main news writers. They are in a hurry, especially in the evenings, when the news development gathers momentum. The copy written by them under pressure is bound to carry errors of all types. In any newspapers, there is always a shortage of space for all news items, which are received in the office. The newspaper's advertisement department is ever eager to grab the valuable but limited space. Moreover, newsprint and means of production cost a lot of money. Ultimately, a newspaper's success largely depends on the space and its most efficient, judicious and economic use. Hence, within the space set aside for news, as much news as possible needs to be packed to serve a divergent readership. Considering these factors, editing of the news copy become essential.

Q2. Define newsroom. What are the characteristics of news?

Ans. A newsroom can be defined as "an office at a television or radio station or a newspaper where news is gathered and reports are prepared for broadcasting or publishing". The newsroom is where the stories are gathered, written, put together, edited and assembled for the news broadcast, telecast or newspaper.

The news room is the centre of all activities in a news organization. The Editorial Department, also called the Editorial Desk or Copy Desk or News Desk, is the nerve centre of a newsroom. At the Editorial Desk, the newspaper issues are planned and made. In a newspaper, in the newsroom, Assistant Editors, News Editors, Chief Sub-Editors, Senior Sub-Editors and Sub-Editors edit copies and place them in pages. Sub-editors also design pages and give headlines. After that the pages are checked by two/three senior person to make sure that the pages do not have any errors.

In news agencies, the news desk is the final stop before a story is sent to the transmission room or creed room for transmission on the wires. In news agencies, desk persons edit copies after they receive from reporters and send them to the creed room for transmission. These days, the process has been computerized. So a sub-editor/senior sub-editor/chief sub-editor transmits the copy.

Desk Management: A desk editor works in a print or broadcast journalism newsroom to gather news tips, assign stories to writers and reporters, and edit the final product before publication or broadcast.

The designation varies according to the choice of the organisation. He plans and directs the day's news operations. He is supported by a team consisting of the news editors, chief sub-editors (chief sub), senior sub-editors and sub-editors (sub).

The news desk usually operates in three shifts: morning, afternoon and night (till late in the evening, even up to 2.30 a.m.). In between, there are two link shifts-morning and evening-which are headed by the news editors and or chief subs. They are also called 'slot' men. Ideally, in a newspaper, it is the news editor who plans and directs page-making, while the chief sub helps and implements it.

In a news agency, news editors and chief subs looks after the smooth functioning of the news desk. They plan and write "leads" (updated versions of developing stories). Here, there is an additional shift called

"Extra Night" (from 2 a.m to 8 a.m.), which is managed by a senior sub-editor.

News Making: There are some characteristics of a news story. Proximity, timeliness, prominence, consequence and human interests are five conventional determinants a news item:

(1) Proximity: The closer the origin of news, the more is its impact. For instance, on a particular day, there is 45 deaths in a bomb blast in South Africa and local bomb blast that kills five people. The local bomb blast will have more impact on the readers.

(2) Timeliness: The more recent its happening, the more worthy it is. News grows old quickly. It perishes fast. However, an event that happened six months back, but is discovered and reported now could grab the front page. For example, the 2G scam and cash-for-vote case which were discovered later on.

(3) Prominence: A famous person makes news and the newspapers like to use as many famous persons as possible. For example, if the Vice-chancellor of a university gets hurt while playing cricket, few people will take note of the incident. But, if a person like Sachin Tendulkar is injured, all the newspapers will carry that.

(4) Consequence: Readers take interest in an event or occurrence which affects him or if he takes part in the event. He takes more interest to know how affects him and his family. For instance, weather stories attract high readership. A storm or cyclone that leaves behind some casualties and causes heavy damage in a town or city will receive better coverage and attract large readership. A raise in the prices of petrol, cooking gas, milk or an increase in water and electricity tariffs will have major impact.

(5) Human Interest: Any interesting story about people and their peculiarities make news and newspapers carry those stories. The human interest stories are little things that have happened, or could happen to yourself or your neighbours or friends. In strict sense, these stories are worth little or nothing as news, yet these are worth telling. For example, a three-month-old baby girl found abandoned in a railway station. Such a story interests the readers. Besides these five elements, there are various other features that could come into play in judging the news:

(i) To become newsworthy, a story must interest a large number of readers.

(ii) A story's worth is determined by its impact on the people. For that reason, the functioning of the government and the politicians receive a lot of coverage. Scientific discoveries find space in the newspapers. For instance, any step toward the cure of cancer or AIDS is sure to generate headlines. Archaeological findings, relating the present to the past, also make news. Accidents, accords, pacts, announcements, business, crime, cultural events, disasters, education, elections, environment, fashion, health, labour, obituaries and tragedies make news.

Editing a Copy: There is a need to read every story, preferably thrice-once for familiarisation, once while we edit, and the third time to check our work. If the story has no glaring problems, and if you fully understand it, you would be ready to edit it. Now, we are concerned with spelling, punctuation, grammar, consciousness of expression, smoothness of writing, general accuracy and comprehensibility.

Format: A news story is divided in to two parts-the opening para called the "intro" (introduction) or the "lead", and the body. The lead describes, simply and briefly, what happened. The body documents and elaborates the lead.

Adequate attention should be paid to the lead, the most vital part of the story. Written in a single sentence, it should grab the reader and compel him to read the body. Normally, the lead is in about 25 words, or may be less. At the maximum, it should be limited to 40 words. The intro should be concise and crisp. It should not meander or puzzle the reader, but summarise the story. Details should be dispersed and blended in the subsequent paragraphs.

Opening Para: Usually the news story has followed the "inverted pyramid" structure. The most significant information is placed at the top, the story's beginning and other details follow in their order of importance. Thus, the story tapers to smaller and smaller details, until it disappears. It may begin with the five Ws and one H, i.e., the who-what-why-when-where and how lead. Basically, a news story should answer what, when and where. The answers should find place in the opening para. The three other questions- who, why and how- do not necessarily arise in all the news copy. In case they do, the answers are accommodated in the subsequent paras. Each succeeding para should add an essential detail without being dependent in content or style on what follows.

The inverted pyramid style enables

(1) A new story, to be self-contained, even if paras are deleted at the bottom due to space; shortage [consequently, a coherent story is left at each point where it could be cut];

(2) A hurried reader to skip over many stories in a short time by just reading the opening paras [those with greater interest could read a story completely];

(3) A sub-editor, to write the headline gets in the gist in the first few paras; and

(4) A sub-editor to change the order of paras or insert new material, even after the matter has been sent to the press for composing.

Rewriting: The sub-editor should, look for errors in spelling, grammar and syntax, and correct these and 'pass' the copy mail editing the story instant second look might sometimes compel him/her to rewrite it. The opening para may lack the punch, or the copy may seem confusing, or the news may be hidden below. Hence, rewriting may become necessary for the sake of clarity. Highlight the news point, taking care to avoid distortion and respect the facts produced by the reporter. Sometimes, the reports obtain the information but fail to exploit it. This could happen particularly when reporting the press conferences and disasters.

Q3. Discuss about Headlines and Leads of news.

Ans. Headlines provide the readers with the optimal ratio between contextual effect and processing effort, and direct readers to construct the optimal context for interpretation.

It is the most vulnerable element in a newspaper. The headline draws the attention of the readers. It compels the reader to read the story. It tells the reader what the story is all about. The headline sells the story.

In a newspaper, the size of the headline shows the importance of a story. The larger or the bolder the headline the most important is the news story. The lead stories in a newspaper generally have bigger headlines than the stories in middle or lower part of the page.

Writing a headline is like applying the finishing polish on a well-crafted piece of furniture. While writing headlines, sub-editors should keep the following points in mind:

- Headlines should inform, educate and entertain the reader
- Headlines should convey the essence of the story.

- Headlines should draw reader's attention and compel the reader to read the story.
- Headlines should be sharp, active and positive,
- Headlines should be written in present tense.
- Commonly-known abbreviations should be used in headlines; Do not use unknown abbreviations in headlines.

For Example: Do not use "Min" for "ministry", "doc" for "doctor", "Af" for "Afghanistan", "engg" for "engineers".

- Do not split a name between two lines: For example,

  Do not write like

  Prime Minister Manmohan

  Singh meets Pakistan President
- Use single quotation (" ") marks in headlines. Double Quotation marks (" ") take more space. Also, single quotation marks are also more attractive.
- Do not use articles "the", "an" and "a" in headlines.

Kicker: Kicker is a one-line heading with a second line above it in a different style, generally half the type size. Kicker headlines are used to dress up a page. Kicker looks like as given below.

THE BOTTOM IS THE MAIN HEADLINE

Hammer: It is the reverse of kicker. It is usually written in all capital letters. The smaller type is the main headline and the big type is the kicker (hammer). Hammer will be one or two word. Hammer looks like as given below.

HAMMER

The main headline

Leads: A lead is a device, mainly used by news agencies, in the case of developing stories for updating the story with additional information. This lead is different from the lead of a news story. News agencies transmit news round the clock. Whenever there is a news break, they transmit it as quick as possible. So as the story develops they send leads of that story. There will be "FIRST LEAR", SECOND LEAD", "THIRD LEAD" and so on. "LEAD ALL" is sent at the end.

A lead is also used to tighten the loose ends in a dispersed story. A lead story is also sent to combine related developments on a particular occasion like Independence Day or Republic Day, or some festivals.

Q4. Who is copy editor? "Sub-editor is the backbone of a newspaper". Why has this saying secured acceptance?

Ans. A writer and a copy editor working together should strive to achieve that goal in every story. The copy editor works to improve the clarity, logic and consistency of the writer's sentences and paragraphs. To produce stories that respect the reader's interests and intelligences, the copy editor must discuss the story at many stages of the writing process. A good copy editor may not be the best writer on a staff but must be someone who understands the elements of good writing.

A copy editor or sub-editor is a bridge between a reporter and the reader. He/she has divergent roles to perform, and does one or more of these tasks while editing (subbing) a copy. He/she need not execute all these functions simultaneously. But, on any given day, he/she will be required to play all these roles.

A copy editor, generally known as the sub-editor or desk person, is a gatekeeper and image builder who protects a newspaper's reputation. It is the responsibility of a sub-editor to convert raw-product into a finished product. He is the person who gives the shape to a newspaper. The material received from a writer comes to the sub-editor for editing. The task of editing includes all the works related to certifying the authenticity of the facts and truth and the style of the newspaper. It is this reason that a sub-editor is called the backbone of a newspaper. He is the person who received the description of news that makes necessary correction or pruning, corrects the language and allots headings to each news before it is sent for publication. The appointment of a sub-editor is the first step of the ladder of appointments on the profession of journalism. In the Indian newspapers, the reporters and the subeditors enjoy the same status. The sub-editors who are engaged in the job of collection of news are called reporters and the sub-editors setting on the copy desk are called the copy-editors. The works of the sub-editors are supervised by the Chief Sub-Editor, who is under the news editor.

Duties of a Copy Editor: Copy editors begin the editing process by fixing any grammatical, punctuation and spelling errors. They also double check that names, places and organizations are spelled properly and that facts, dates and statistics are accurate. This may involve contacting writers' sources and conducting online research. Copy editors also write headlines and subheads for articles and, depending on the publication, create page layouts that consist of the placement of articles, photographs and advertisements.

Each publication employs its own style guide that dictates writing standards, such as tense, voice or the spelling of certain words. Copy editors ensure that articles are written in accordance with the style guide. They work closely with writers, suggesting changes to enhance articles' readability, conciseness and style. Copy editors also help writers research topics and locate and contact sources throughout the development of articles.

A reader who scans through his morning newspaper is in a great hurry. Hence, a copy editor should carve out each story in a familiar language so that it runs smoothly the average reader's mind. Smooth writing ensures smooth reading. Simple, direct sentences are more directive. Also he/she should delete cliches, extraneous works, jargon, ambiguities, non-descript adjectives and adverbs.

Rewrites and restructures stories extensively, where necessary. As far as possible, the sub (editor) should look for errors in spelling, grammar and syntax, and clear the copy. But, an instant second look may sometimes compel him/her to rewrite it. The opening para may lack the punch, the copy may seem confusing, or the news may be hidden below. Hence, rewriting may become necessary for the sake of clarity.

Highlight the news-point, taking care to avoid distortion and respect the facts produced by the reporter. In case the copy is badly written, show it to the reporter. Sometimes, the reporters obtain the information, and fail to exploit it. This could happen while reporting the press conferences and major tragedies such as plane or train accidents.

Deletes doubtful words and sentences, following the thumb rule "when in doubt, leave out". Every story does not require all these treatment. But, every day, some story or the other will require any or most of these operations; a sub frequently performs these functions.

A copy editor/sub-editor should make sure that words are spelt correctly. A spelling error is a major error, and reflects badly on the credibility of a newspaper. A few moments spent on checking the spelling of a word will keep the reader's mind at ease.

The main functions of a sub-editor are as under:

(1) Administrative Work:

(i) Giving directions to the compositors and printers.

(ii) Control of the press copy. Utilization of the material according to the availability of space.

(iii) Making ready the miller or type copy.

(2) Creative Works: Examining the news, collection and proper presentation of the news and allotment of headlines.

(3) Points to be Noted by a Sub-Editor:

(i) Use of correct language.

(ii) Avoiding grammatical mistakes.

(iii) Simple structure of sentences.

(iv) Style of the newspaper to be attractive and should confirm to the standard of the newspaper

(v) Use of obscene and uncivil words to be avoided.

(vi) The facts should be examined and verified.

(vii) The views should be free from any prejudice.

(viii)Dry language should be avoided.

(ix) All the important facts should be included.

(x) A news should not be false, old, irrelevant and advertisement.

(xi) A news should not attract any legal complications in the future.

(xii) A news should not attract any legal complications in the future.

(xiii)There should be no repetition of an old news and it should not be motivated any sense of revenge

(xiv)The heading should be clear and meaningful.

(xv) The heading should be worded properly and should be based on the facts.

(xvi)The heading should itself give the gist of the news matter.

A sub-editor is called a publisher's hack and a mutilator, because he does the pruning of the press copy; he has to give suitable headlines and where necessary, revise and condense the material to suit the available space. Based on these facts, it is said that he mutilates even a best story sent by a reporter; that could be the reason that he is called a publisher's hack.

Q5. What are the qualities and tools that are essential in a copy editor/sub editor?

Ans. The essential qualities of a copy editor/sub-editor are as follows:

- **Calmness:** S/he should be calm and composed whatever may the situation. S/he should not get excited when a big story breaks–be it a disaster, calamity, the assassination of a big political leader or the collapse of a government.
- **Decisive:** Take quick and correct decisions. The editorial department has no place for indecisives.
- **Non-partisan:** Never take sides; be non-partisan.
- **Memory:**S/he should have a sharp memory for counter-checking facts, if necessary.
- **Grasp:** Size up the situation as it unfolds and estimate its relevance.
- **Know your reader:** Know the particular readership. This means s/he should engage one hand with subbing and the other with the pulse of the reader.
- **Self-confidence:** S/he need to have confidence enough to correct a bad copy written by anyone, even the senior most reporter or the paper's editor.
- **Mature:** S/he should be mature enough to correct only bad copy and not just make changes for the sake of changing.
- **Sceptical:** Do not accept anything at face value. S/he should approach everything as a source of potential error.
- **Knowledge:** Be a jack of all trades, because a sub handles a wide range of stories (from killings to oil prices of satellite launch). S/he has to handle varieties of news stories and need to have knowledge on everything. A good editor should store most of the information as it comes across, and search for more.
- **Stability:** Have enough stability to work under pressure.

Essential tools of copy/sub editors are the copy editor will require a set of tools, the lack of which may lead to loss valuable time while subbing the copy. These aids are indispensable. Often, s/he may come across problems of spellings and facts, arising out of an average day's handing of the news. S/he should focus on the errors, and correct the name. a list of references shall include:

- A standard unabridged dictionary, English–English, Mother tongue–English;
- A book on who's who;

- A good atlas;
- Maps–India and World;
- Indian Constitution;
- Style book;
- Police laws;
- Press laws;
- Library or morgue with clippings files;
- Roget's thesaurus;
- An encyclopaedia;
- List of council of ministers at the Centre;
- List of MPs in the Lok Sabha and Rajya Sabha; and
- H. W. Flower's Modern English Usage.

Q6. What are the editing marks and symbols?

Ans. The professional way to edit is by having a copy editor find errors, mark them and expect the reporter to make the changes indicated.

- **Slug:** Slug is identification mark or tag. It is generally used by news agencies. A news agency may transmit a number of stories on the same subject. So a similar slug will show that these stories are connected. For example, in case of a bomb blast, "BLAST" will be the mast slug and each related story will have this slug. Suppose there is a toll story then the sub slug of that story will be "BLAST-TOLL". Suppose there is a reaction of the Prime Minister over the blast, the sub slug of the story will be "BLAST-PM". Also, if the story is too long and has been split into two or more parts, the slug gets numbered. For example, The "BLAST-PM" be "BLAST-PM ONE" and "BLAST-PM TWO".
- **Editing Symbols:** A journalist should know these symbols for editing a copy. No only desk person but reporters should have knowledge about these symbols. Sometimes reporters may have to edit his copies.

Q7. What is Photo Editing? What are the essential features of Newspaper Photographer?

Ans. Picture submitted for publication in the newspapers and magazines have to be edited to fit into the layout of the page and also the unnecessary portions cut off, which the photographer might have added in the actual composition. The competent picture editor's main work is to see that he does not waste space and trims a picture keeping the main essence of the subject intact.

A good picture editor working carefully with the other photographers and designers can make a big difference to a publication. Unfortunately, many staff appoint a photo editor without training that persons to do the job. Photo editors should be present at all staff meetings and contribute to the discussion of story development and planning. They should help writers develop photo assignments that will contribute to the story development. These assignments should be realistic for photographers to complete and should avoid staged, posed or predictable images. Photo editors should tailor used. Photographers should use picture-editing software to complete basic picture alterations such as toning, burning, dodging and cropping. Other alterations may be used to correct crooked horizon lines or redeye.

Photo editors should look at layouts with designers when complete to make sure visual variety has been achieved in chosen photographs with photo angles, lens use, the number of people in each picture, cropping and in the actual content in the images. The photo editor can also check for consistency in toning.

Features of the Newspaper Photographer: The value of a photograph as a means of communication has been long accepted all over the journalistic world. A photograph needs no words–except perhaps for a brief identifying caption. Even an illiterate person can 'read' something from a picture. Research has shown that most newspaper readers recall more easily the main news picture on a particular day than that day's most widely read news story.

It is not only the photographs but also any illustration, diagram, map, cartoon or line drawing– which can be an important communication tool. A newspaper photographer has long been recognised as a journalist in his own right. He must be skilled not only in the handling of a camera; he needs the insight and experience to be at the right place at the right time– to "get the story" through his camera lens. He is generally briefed at the office beforehand on the type of photograph required. A press photographer, in addition to the pictures, also provides a caption giving details of the subject matter.

In editing photographs, the aim should be to increase the visual impact. Just as a skilful sub-editor may brighten a dull piece of writing, imaginative editing can transform a disappointing print into an interesting picture. A picture must be judged not only on its technical excellence–bright, sharp, well composed, but also on its news value. The newsworthiness, and whether it conforms to accepted standards of honest reporting and good taste, should be the main considerations in evaluating the relevance of a picture.

Q8. Define the professionalism of Photo Editor. Identify the main qualities of a good photographer.

Ans. Pictures are in everything around us. Each one of us sees different pictures in the same object and situations, owing to the different background and experience each of us have. It is the job of the photo editor to select the best photograph which tells the story on its own. The photo editor edits it to suit the space in the page without destroying or distorting the essence of the picture and gives it a good display.

A good photo editor always takes the photographers into confidence, holding frequent discussions with them from the time assignments are given to them till the final outcome of the photograph on the photo editor's desk. It is the duty of photo editor to give the photographers ideas about the picture possibilities. While the photographers are in the dark room with the enlarger, he joins them in composing the picture on the easel board, which saves a lot of time and leaves no ill feeling with the photographers. Photographers hate most when the picture is trimmed and edited in their absence.

(1) Qualities of a Good Photographer: The quality of a photograph depends on its composition, although, the composition of a photograph depends on the photographer's vision, creativity and expertise in capturing the reality in photo. Photographer has to work with great speed on a location. On location, no one will wait while he tries to figure out his shutter and lens aperture adjustment in his camera. Even as he takes out his vehicle, he should be setting his aperture for the type of lighting available on the location or what he intend to use (like an electronic flash) and be ready to focus to an average distance.

Photograph should actually shoot a news event from several different angles, and let his photo editor decide which picture to use. But when everything starts happening, at the same time, he must be quick enough to do his own editing on the spot. His grasping power must be like quick silver. He must decide which picture from what angle would be the best and then get himself position in to shoot it.

The newspaper photographs are based on factual situation. The photographs illustrates an event, bring depth into it, and probably comment on it. Usually, the photographer is given only an idea to work with, and is expected to create an appropriate photograph to illustrate it. This is where a good memory or a notebook will come in handy. The photographic techniques involved in shooting for magazines are not much different from those in newspapers.

(2) Going about a Story: When someone is assigned to take photos of any news event, s/he should reach the spot before the scheduled time. Focus on the subject and be creative. A photo must tell the story. Take as many pictures (about dozen or more than that) as possible. Sometime s/he would be surprised to find that only two or three photos out of the hundred even come close to being good pictures. Do not be discouraged. This is not a bad average, even for a professional. That is why the professionals shoot dozens and dozens of rolls on a single assignment. If there are not many good shots this time, there will be more the next time and, who knows s/he might be closer to his/her goal.

Q9. Discuss about "Creative Cropping of Pictures" in Photo Editing.

Ans. Cropping means to trim the unnecessary portions of an image's outer area; it is one of the easiest ways to enhance an image. Cropping need not be a radical change; it might simply remove unwanted details from the edges of the frame. An overly broad or busy scene can be distracting and frustrating—the viewer does not know where to look at first. The intelligent photo editor adopt different creative cropping techniques to bring out the exact point of emphasis a 'pix' (a term used for picture). They try to enlarge the main image, which will have a better visual impact.

For Example: The first step in editing the eagle photo is to crop, or cut away, some of the extra sky and branches so the photo focuses on the eagle. Photographers try to compose and capture images full-frame, which means the object of interest fills the dimensions of the photo. When that is not possible, photographers and graphic artists crop the photo either to create an illusion of full-frame, to fit unusual shapes in layouts, or to make the image more dramatic. From a design point of view, sometimes it is necessary to crop a photo to straighten an image, remove distracting elements, or simplify the subject. The goal of most cropping is to make the most important feature in the original photo stand out. Cropping sometimes is used to convert a digital photo's proportions to those typical for traditional photos.

Many a time, the photographers do their job mechanically, giving relevance only to technical qualities, and having no instinct for news. A photo editor, who keeps track of the news, also highlights the portion in the photograph which has news value.

A photo editor studies the picture carefully, and decides about the cropping. First, he crops the picture mentally (visualizing how it would look like), and then decides on the final edited photograph. A badly cropped pix cannot be repaired, and the person who does such a job for the cropping sake gets the nick name of 'a butcher'.

Q10. Write short notes on the following:

(i) Choosing a Picture

Ans. The photographer may submit multiple pictures of a news event it is the photo editor's task to select the best photos. The editor also takes pix from freelance photographer if he does not find suitable pictures. The selected photos should be appealing and should enhance the beauty of the page. In newspapers the photographers leave contact sheets with the photo editor to enable him to choose the right frame and mark the composition.

(ii) Graphic Illustrations

Ans. Illustrator is known primarily for being a vector-drawing program over an image-editing program. Vector graphics are images that are composed of mathematically defined geometric shapes, lines, paths, objects and fills. Images created in Photoshop are comprised of pixels.

Graphic illustrations are used in newspapers and magazines to detail the activities that took place at a spot or to narrate the incidents how it happened. It is needed because photos cannot show the details. Also in most news coverage, the photographer reaches the spot only after the incident takes place and takes photos of results or what has happened. So news editors decide to take graphic illustrations.

From the information available, the entire incident in sequence could be sketched out so as to give the reader a clear idea of what the news story is about. Such graphic illustrations have been used by newspapers and magazines very often.

In a crime, a graphic illustration could show the position of the criminals involved in it, the victims, the police and others in sequel with timings. Tabloids and magazines use lots of graphic illustrations along with the detailed stories.

(iii) Computer Applications in Photo Editing

Ans. A very important aspect of computer application in photo editing is that the picture quality in terms of tones, density, colour sharpness and so on could be reproduced to near perfection, which was not always possible in the previous conventional methods. This also applies to the 'Photo Fax', where photographs are faxed from outstations and are transmitted directly to the computer, from where all necessary adjustments could be made. Photos could be stored and recalled on the computer as and when required.

The latest technology enables one to use sophisticated equipment for photo editing. The selected negatives are scanned, the contrast adjusted, and the picture cropped on the computer video display terminal as required. Then, the image is directly transferred to the page. The elimination of the intermediary procedures, used in the conventional system until now, avoids handling of the negatives or transparencies, thus making sure that the reproduction is of a class.

Q11. Describe various composing methods in technological developments.

Ans. Until the 19th century, Gutenberg's print technology had not changed dramatically. In the early 1800's the development of continuous rolls of paper, a steam-powered press and a way to use iron instead of wood for building presses all added to the efficiency of printing. These technological advances made it possible for newspaperman Benjamin Day to drop the price of his New York Sun to a penny a copy in 1833. Some historians point to this "penny press" as the first true mass medium--in Day's words, his paper was designed to "lay before the public, at a price well within the means of everyone, all the news of the day."

(1) Technological Developments: Major changes have occurred in newspaper composing and printing methods these are as follows:

(i) **Hand Setting:** It is also called hand composing. Hand setting is the original method of typesetting. It is still used extensively.

This is done by manually. The typesetter uses a composing stick, a type case and the metal type. The compositor holds the composing stick in one hand and picks type from the case with the other. To provide the desired amount of leading or space between lines, metal strips called leads. After the composing stick is completed, the lines of types are set in a long shallow tray, called "galley."

After proofreading and the necessary corrections are made, the next step is to make-up the page. In page makeup, various elements like the text type, display type and picture blocks are set as per the designed layout.

Since the composed matter consists of hundreds of individual pieces, it is essential that it is held together securely or locked up. This may be done by typing up the type with a string or by surrounding with furniture strips of wood, metal or plastic are used for typing up the type in a metal frame, called a "chase" or directly on the bed of the press. The types and other printed matter ready to be printed is called a "forme."

(ii) **Machine Setting:** This method of type setting is also called hot type as in this types are set from molten metal. There are mainly four types of casting machines-Linotype, Intertype, Monotype and Ludlow.

Linotype and intertype are mechanical process of composing and casting type in one piece lines called "slugs". As these machines cast lines and not individual characters, they are called line-casting machines.

(a) **Linotype and Intertype:** Linotype machine was invented by Ottmar Mergenthaler, a German by birth, in America in 1885 and the Inter type was produced by Herman Ridder, publisher of the New York Staats Zeitung, and was put into operation at the New York Journal of Commerce in 1913. The 'Linotype' and its substantially identical competitor the Intertype are mechanical type setting machines that cast lines of type characters as solid metal slugs. These machines were universally used for setting newspapers. The range of type sizes available on slug casting machine varied according to their models. The normal range was $4^1/_2$ pt. to 48 pt. The maximum width of slug which could be cast was 36 pica ems.

In Linotype and intertype, the operator adjusts keys and the machine to set type to the desired pica measure and leading. The upper front section of the machine carries a magazine, a slotted metal container, which holds the letter moulds, called matrices, of the type to be set.

The operator strikes the keys to form a line-of-type with the matrices. Characters and wedged-shaped space bands are created within the given line measure. To create word space, the space hands are used. When the operator is ready to cast a line, he pulls a lever which triggers a series of events. The line is transferred to the casting mechanism. The wedge-shaped space bands are driven up between the words to justify the line. Molten metal is forced into the matrices, the trimmed line of type of slug is ejected onto a pan or galley tray. With the help of a mechanical distributor, the matrices are returned to the magazine and the space bands to the space-band box soon after the type is cast.

After the matter is composed, the type lines are locked in a galley. Once the type has been cast, it is impossible to reduce the amount of leading as line-casting machines sets type and leading as one piece. Leading can be increased by inserting leads between lines by hand. Any change within a line means that the entire line or even all the succeeding lines in a paragraph have to be reset. The difference between intertype and linotype is that the intertype of matrices can be used for casting headlines as well as body matter.

(b) **Monotype:** The original Monotype system consisted of a Composition Caster and separate keyboard, but over time, the Lanston Monotype Machine Corporation created a number of machines based on similar principles that expanded the range of type sizes that could be cast in-plant, as well as perfecting the free-standing Material Maker for leading, rule and fancy borders. In this method, the characters are cast one by one rather as a complete line. Two machines are used in this method-a keyboard or perforator and a type caster. It is thus called two-step or two-machine method of casting characters. The operator adjusts the machine to the required pica measure and leading. As the copy is typed, it produces a perforated paper roll, which is used to drive the type caster. A combination of holes dictates the letters, spaces and punctuation marks. A normal spacing is punched in to the roll between words. A calculator measure the amount of unused space at the end of the line and the operators then punches the holes to indicate the amount of additional space to be given between words to justify the line.

When the roll is fed into the casting machine, it is fed in backwards so that the machine "memorises" the amount of space to be added between words as the letters are cast. To set type, the perforated roll is fitted on the type caster, where it directs the casting mechanism by means of compressed air. The air passing through the perforations brings the matrix holder and specific matrix ready to be filled with molten metal into proper position. Once the type is cast, it is ejected onto a galley.

(c) **Ludlow:** It is typically cast on a fixed point size body. In this method, both hand setting and machine-casting are used. A slug is produced like in linotype method, but in a different way. The operator sets the type matrices and leading in a composing stick by hand. The composed matrices are then locked into a casting machine, where they are filled with molten lead to produce the slug. Ludlow was primarily used to cast display type from 12 to 72 points and mainly forth headlines of a newspaper.

(iii) **Phototypesetting:** It is different from the hot metal casting method. In the first phase, it is like monotype setting and involves a cold type process. If the perforator is not attached to a Video Display Unit (VDU), the operation is limited to conversion of copy matter into a coded perforated tape. The perforated tape is then fed into a coded perforated tape. The perforated tape is then fit into a programmed computerized unit, which projects the desired images of type characters onto photosensitive film or paper. This paper is then made up in mechanicals or photo mechanicals from which printing plates can be produce. It is a fast, flexible and reasonably economical method of typesetting. In this method, there are several advantages over other methods. In this process, individual letters are projected and exposed directly on to photosensitive paper of film, resulting in the sharpest possible letter forms.

In this process, the type can be set and mater made up directly on photosensitized film or paper. Thus, it is possible to go directly from film to plate-making. This process saves time for the designer as well as the printer. A phototypesetting unit with a visual display terminal offers the additional advantage of providing a visual display of the composed matter. Phototypesetting is done through the computers which carry out programmed decisions and eliminate errors caused by human judgement. Thus, it reduces pre-press time.

(iv) By Computer: A computer can be programmed to perform all the calculation required to set up word-spacing within acceptable limits. Photo editing and page designing can also be done on the computers. Now all newspapers are using computers for composing and other pre-press works.

The computer contains, within its stored programme, all or most of the typographical decisions an experienced compositor takes as a result of his knowledge and experience in typesetting. The programme may be written to produce the required kind of text-setting. The output of the computer-coded paper tape can be used to control the actual typesetting equipment, including the conventional automatic composing machines using hot metal or any phototypesetting system. The outcome of the total system is dependent on the computer programme employed.

A computer can be programmed to carry out all the calculation needed to establish work-spacing within acceptable limits, and, beyond these, a work-break is required to break up a work and place part of it in the next line. Photo editing and page designing can also be done on the computers. Now-a-days, almost all big newspapers in India are using the computers for composing purposes.

(2) Market-Readership Changes: Different editorial components of a daily newspaper or a magazine are generally news reports, special reports, photographs, book reviews, art reviews, film reviews, feature articles, interview stories, investigative and interpretative reports. Along with these, newspapers also publish advertisements, with display and classified public information, notices and jobs/employment advertisements. In addition, newspapers also publish the stock market information, weather reports, radio, television, cinema and theatre charts.

The newspapers operate in a competitive world. In addition, these have to compete with the radio and television.

Also, as living styles and product consumption patterns of the readers improve, the newspaper editors and proprietors have to improve the quality of their product. Therefore, to keep up with the times, there has been a marked improvement in the use of the typography and newspaper design in the newspapers during the last few years. More improvements are bound to take place with innovations in newspaper production. If we take a closer look at the newspapers being published from different centres in India, we will notice many differences in their use of typography, design and production techniques. Several newspapers have started using colour printing for improving their appeal to the advertisers and readers.

(3) Newspapers Today – Design and Contents: Newspapers come in different shapes and size. Some newspapers are broadsheets and some of the papers are tabloids. They have different typography. 'The Times of India' is different from 'The Indian Express'. 'The Hindu' is different from 'The Hindustan Times'. They have their unique look and design. The papers are also different contents. Some newspapers are exclusively for business news. Every newspaper has its own way of presenting news and articles. The newspapers of different cities have different priorities in news coverage. Kolkata newspapers include local Kolkata stories on the front page, while Chennai papers include Chennai local stories on the page one. This is because their target readers are different.

(4) Newspapers Sizes and Formats: Daily newspapers come in different sizes. Some of the papers come in broadsheet while some newspapers are printed in tabloids. Even broadsheet newspapers have different sizes may be it is because of their printing requirements. 'The Hindu', 'The Indian Express' and 'The Times of India' are bigger in width relative to 'The Hindustan Times'. 'Mail Today' and 'Mint' come in tabloid size. These two are tabloids, yet they are different in sizes. These papers have different looks. Their Mast heads have unique looks. Their fonts and type sizes are different. They have their own unique style.

Q12. Discuss the concept of Daily Newspaper. Also, explain various components included in this.

Ans. A daily newspaper is issued every day, sometimes with the exception of Sundays and occasionally Saturdays and often of some national holidays. The front page is the face of a newspaper. Front page is normally read first by the readers. It draws the attention of the readers. Newspapers also design their front pages attractively. No other page of a newspaper looks like the front page. The front page shows the qualities and identity of a paper. All the important news of the day are carried on the page one. Most of the newspapers carry three/four big stories in the front page and some important news are given in brief in a column on the front page. Some newspapers also carry whether report in brief, stock market indices and gold and silver rates on the page.

(1) Newspaper Identity: The front page of a newspaper is like the face of a person. The front page is the identity of a newspaper. Every newspaper has different types of masthead. If we compare the front page of two newspapers, take for example, 'The Times of India' and 'The Indian Express', we will find that they have different sizes of masthead. 'The Times of India's' front page is divided into eight columns while 'The Indian Express' has six columns. They use different fonts and types sizes for headlines and body copies of news stories. Every newspaper has some typical features on their front page.

(2) The Masthead: The name of the newspaper written in big fonts on the top of the front page is called Masthead. All newspapers write the Masthead in big fonts. They are generally bold. Some newspapers have masthead written in simple format, some newspaper use style and italic fonts.

(3) The Headlines: The headlines are the important in a newspaper. They draw the attention to the readers. Many newspaper readers read only headlines. Headlines also compel a reader to read the story.Each headline is a new and unique challenge for a page designer. The headlines for him are much more than just a set of words. The page designer is responsible to make each headline as distinct as possible within the given newspaper format. On a particular page, each headline has different font and different type size.

A headline can be a single line and run horizontally across columns or two lines. We can see the difference clearly if we open a page. Each page designer uses his own experience and creative genius to make the page attractive and give each news item an appropriate placement on the page.

(4) Placement of Photographs and Cartoons: Photographs, cartoons and graphics have special significance in a newspaper; they improve the look of a paper. They provide aesthetic appeal of a newspaper. Placing a picture or cartoon at wrong place may not only reduce its utility, but also reduce the design appeal of the total page. Photos and illustrations are evaluated on the basis of their subject-matter, topicality, clarity and news value. The page designer has to see whether picture has independent news value or has to be juxtaposed with a particular news story. Their size needs adjustment because of the space constraint.

(5) Overall Page Design: Offset printing is the most commonly used reproduction system for all media and has impacted design in newspapers overall. Every newspaper has his own unique design. No two newspapers are the same. Some newspapers carry cartoons in the front page. Some newspapers have pointers under the Masthead. Some newspapers have table and graphic illustrations on the Front page. Some newspapers have single column story along with four/five three/ four column stories. They are unique in their own look.]

Q13. Describe how the Inside Pages are different from the front page of the daily newspapers.

Ans. Inside pages are different from front page in design, format, structure and presentation of contents. Inside pages have title as per the topics covered on that page-City, Region, State, International, Trends, Editorial, Business and Sport. The news stories on a particular inside pages generally have a common link. It helps the readers in their search for news items. Grouping of news item also provide the newspaper a structure.

(1) The Editorial Page: Normally every newspaper has an editorial page. On this page, there will be two/three write-ups, generally comments on different current national or international topics. These are generally the voice of the newspaper. Editorial page also carries one or two articles either written by a staff write or freelancers. The page also carries "Letters to the editor."

Each newspaper has, usually, a fixed spot for general information items such as the weather forecast, entertainment, cinema, radio, television, etc. The design of the inside pages of a newspaper is relatively much more structured than the front page, which is dependent on the major happenings during the past few hours.

(2) Advertisements: All newspapers and magazines are the main source of revenue for them because these commercial ads. There are different types of advertisements and classified. Newspapers have different price for these ads. The front page advertisements cost more than inside pages. The cost also increases if the ad size increases. Thus, a full page ad has more cost than a half page advertisements. Some newspapers have also special supplements for advertisements and classifieds.

(3) Readability and Overall Appeal: Newspapers are meant for reading. The person who is making page should try to improve the readability of a page. Anything that hinders the readability of a page should be removed. Each word, each story, headlines, photographs, cartoons, box items, charts and graphics are the important ingredients of the newspaper page design. All these elements are responsible for the readability of a newspaper page. Readability from a page designer's point of view depends on placement of the news stories, typography and the overall page layout.

Q14. What are the periodicals? Write the characteristics of periodicals.

Ans. A periodical is any source that is published at regular intervals, such as daily, weekly, monthly, etc. Journals and magazines, which are considered periodicals, are important sources for up-to-date information in all disciplines. Whether the periodical in question is a newspaper aimed to keep the inhabitants of a city informed about current events or an academic journal designed to keep professionals in a discipline up-to-date on research in the field, periodicals speak to particular audiences at a specific moment in time. Though their news does not stay new for long, their lasting value to historians is in the thorough, idiosyncratic way they give a picture of a particular moment.

(1) Cover Page and its Importance: The cover pages of periodicals have special significance from the editorial and newspaper's policy. While about 85 per cent dailies are subscribed to and delivered at homes or offices, more than 50 per cent magazines are looked at before being bought. Hence, the magazine covers have special significance.

It is the cover of a magazine that holds someone's eyes and makes him/her pick it up and compels to purchase it. Generally, the magazine covers have photographs of women. It is said that the readers like pictures of women on the cover of a magazine, but no cover on the women.

The cover page each magazine issue is real challenge for a page designer. It is a challenge, because the designer is expected to incorporate into the design the following points:

- aesthetic attractiveness;
- colour/variety;
- uniqueness to attract attention;
- an invitation to purchase contents; and
- effective temptation to buy it.

(2) Design Alternatives: Magazines have different designs. There are also alternatives a designer can opt for. There are however a few factors that make some designs more suitable than others.

Magazines very magazines have a pattern for cover page design and that sets the trend or standard for selection of the alternatives which may or may not be suitable for particular magazine. Sometimes magazines experiments with unconventional designs, but too much variation from the past may also tend to alienate the regular readers.

(3) Sales Promotion, Eye-catching Strategies: The success of a magazine is measured by the number of readers willing to pay of it, which can be called paid circulation. For implementing an effective sales promotion strategy, you have know the target readers or the readership profile which is defined in terms of are group, educational level, marital status, disposable income, nature of job, quality, place of residence and consumption pattern. More general interest magazine is read by a wide spectrum of people.

Sales promotion strategy of the publisher or the editor can also effect the price and cover design of a magazine. The cover page of the magazine will be designed accordingly.

Q15. Describe the concept of consistency and change in journalism. What are the factors that must keep in mind while incorporating changes in page make-up or design layout?

Ans. Change is a way of life in journalism. No two editions of a newspaper or magazine are alike. Whenever a reader picks up a newspaper or magazine, he/she expects to find something new in it.

However, in newspapers and magazines, changes take place within the predetermined format. Formats provide a sense of continuity. Format, may be viewed as a rough outline of the newspaper or magazine, its shape and size, placement of its masthead, and the typeface used for it; placement and presentation of the news, views and other contents. Presently change in a continuous manner is the skill that makes design layout a challenge for each item, on each page, of each publication.

Need for Change: At the first glance it may seem obvious that the change is inevitable, so the question of "need" may seem redundant. However, it is essential that we understand the areas of change that influence the very existence of a newspaper of a magazine and also determine its readership growth pattern. While incorporating changes in page make-up or design layout we must keep a few factors:

- While bulk of the readers will remain the same, some new readers, however small, may be added with each new edition.
- Some readers dropout and thus change the overall readership profile.
- Newspapers and magazines operate in a competitive environment, hence new challenges from competitions have to be met.
- Tastes, information requirements and entertainment requirements of readers keep changing.

Handling Last Minute Change: It is uncommon in the newspaper industry that changes have to be incorporated when the total publication is almost ready or at times under print. In daily newspapers it is almost a way of life.

Whenever last minute changes have to be incorporated–the effort is to incorporate the required changes or include the new items with minimum disturbance to the overall page layout. However, some sudden events may warrant total change in the front page layout or cover design of a magazine. Even in case of the most drastic situation, the important factors to be taken note are the time required to bring about the change and the impact of changes on the printing process and schedule. Each printing process and schedule, has its own advantages and limitations. While bringing about changes in the editorial matter their impact on the printing time should also be considered.

Events, which demand last minute changes usually require prominent display.

Q16. What is Typography? Why it is very important in layout and design?

Ans. Typography refers to the use of types. The word 'type' refers to a letter, number, or any other character used in printing. Types are not used just anyhow; wrong use of type could impede communication.

Typography involves careful study, selection, composition and use of types in such a way as to enhance effective communication. Although the phrase 'typographical error' is now often misused, it originally meant an error in typography, most often the use of a wrong type at a point in time. Similarly, typographical pluralism refers to a good combination of types in such a way that an excellent or a visually pleasant pattern is created.

Typography can also be elevated into an art form, and some of the best examples are found in advertising design. For example, most consumers associate particular fonts with certain branded products, because the advertising campaign featured distinctive use of those fonts. The design teams behind the advertising campaign made a series of design roughs that probably included a variety of fonts so that the designers and company executives could decide on a design which best represented the company.

Especially in modern art, typography is also used to convey an artistic statement. Famous works of modern art often include the use of text as a visual medium, sometimes alone and sometimes with image. The font, letter spacing, and color are all important considerations for maximum visual impact. Small changes can radically alter the look and feel of a piece, and many computer graphic design programs make it easier for designers to modify their text to perfection. Classic typography, using movable type and a press, required a close eye to detail, and an ability to extrapolate the final look of the piece from limited visual information.

Historical Perspective: Typography has been witnessing change like everything around us. Scripts which were used forty or fifty years ago look very different from the ones that are in use today for similar publications.

Improvements in typography have come because of technological innovations, competition among the publications as well as changes in reading habits.

Type provides the means for including symbols (letters, numbers and punctuation marks in the printed message. Two basic kinds of type are available for this purpose-hot type and cold type.

Most hot-type composition methods employ type made form molten metal. Each piece of hot type consists of one or more raised characters on a metal body. Hot type can be set by hand (foundry type) or by machine (Monotype, Linotype, Ludlow). After the desired words and sentences have been set, the type is inked and then printed on dull, coated white paper. The resulting print (reproduction proof) serves as the copy used in the photo-offset reproduced process. Metal type is not used in cold-type composition methods. Instead, the copy required for photo-offset reproduction is produced using one or more of the following techniques: It can be hand assembled from preprinted paper and 'plastic letters; it can be set with a typewriter and it can be generated by photographic methods.

Type Faces: The term typeface refers to the unique shape or design of the characters included in a type font, type series, or type family. A font is a complete assortment of characters of a single size and design. It includes uppercase (capital) letters lowercase (small letters) numbers and punctuation marks. The word series is used when referring to a particular type font that is available in more than one size and a family is a group of related, but slightly different type fonts and type series.

Although family members all possess the same general design characteristics, they may differ with regard to the spacing weight, and/or slope of their individual characters. Although thousands of typefaces exist, all can be categorized into six ma or classes or styles. Understanding the characteristics of each style of type will help customer when selecting types for a particular job. The six major type styles are text, roman, sans serif, square serif, script and novelty.

Q17. Discuss the classification of easy and meaningful communication between page designers.

Ans. Classification: To make communication easy and meaningful for page designers, type faces are grouped according to their size and design. Each group, called a family, has been given a name to make the identification easy.

Families: The main features of a family is the style or general shape of its type face as light, medium, bold or heavy. Some of the popular type families are given below. The family names are given in their respective type faces.

Bodoni MT Black
Bodoni MT Black Bold
Bodoni MT Black Italic

Arial Black
Arial Black Bold
Arial Black Italic

Arial
Arial Bold
Arial Italic

Bookman Old Style
Bookman Old Style Bold
Bookman Old Style Italic

Book Antiqua
Book Antiqua Bold
Book Antiqua Italic

Century Gothic
Century Gothic Bold
Century Gothic Italic

Century Schoolbook

Century Schoolbook Bold

Century Schoolbook Italic

Structures and Readability: For a page design, both attractive structures and readability are important. However an attractive structure may or may not be legible. Thus a designer has to keep both the things in mind while designing a page.

Using Typography to Enhance Design: Different type faces have different visual impacts. Each letter has immense potential to be used as a piece of art. A page designer should use his creativity and can be a typographic artist to design the page attractively.

Matching and Contrast: Newspapers now have wider choice in matching and contrasting typefaces after the popularity of Phototype setting and offset printing. However, newspapers use very limited typefaces.

Some newspapers only use one or two. The only variation is the size.

Some newspapers use one bold face of one "Family" for the headlines and type face of another family, usually of smaller size for sub heading. This is a commonly found in magazine design.

Emphasis and Highlights: In a page layout, sometimes you have to emphasise or highlight a word, an expression, a sentence, a paragraph or even a portion of the news item. You can emphasise or highlight in the following ways.

- Use italics face of the fonts
- Use Bold face of the fonts
- Underline the word or sentence

To emphasise a portion, display that part with wider margin, different colour or a combination of above alternative.

Q18. What is electronic editing? Discuss about Electronic Revolution and the Newspaper Industry.

Ans. It is a method of electronically transferring pictures and sound from one videotape to another. This new, or edited, copy is regarded as a second-generation copy. Electronic editing encompasses all changes made to an electronic document written by someone other than the editor. The term electronic editing describes the process of *editing on screen*. On-screen editing is facilitated by advanced software options which give more flexibility in the editing process. Electronic editing has created an extremely valuable field of opportunity for today's editors, allowing for the rapid exchange of edited documentation over great distances. However, every great invention has drawbacks along with the benefits it provides to others.

Electronic Revolution and the Newspaper Industry: Transmission of news has become faster today because of the advanced electronic equipment. Now in few seconds, news can be delivered wherever it may have made the delivery of news very easy. Besides, the speed of the delivery of the information, serious thought is being given to the aesthetic presentation of the textual and visual material on a printed page. This is being treated on par with the editing of information, for both content and language.

The computers and word processors are being used in page make-up. The painstaking manual typesetting and page layouts are a thing of the past. The expertise of the graphic designers and the options made available by the computers have together provided a variety of page designs to choose from.

The facsimile machines, popularly called the 'fax machines,' have proven themselves to be indispensable in reporting back to a newspaper office from the location of an event. These facilitate faster dispatch of news from the newspaper office too. Let us now see what functions the electronic equipment must perform to meet the requirement of the newspaper office.

Q19. What are the requirements of Newsroom? Discuss.

Ans. The number of jobs and people working in the newsroom vary depending on the media outlet. In smaller media outlets, at suburban weekly newspapers for example the newsroom will probably feature only a couple of journalists and a photographer. Sometimes the editor will be there, although in many suburban newspapers the editor has a roving role overseeing a number of newspapers in different offices.

Newsrooms in the past have had vertical and horizontal layers. Newspaper newsrooms have ranged vertically from the editor in-chief at the top to the cub reporter on the bottom. Horizontally, large mainstream newsrooms have produced several types of journalism, both print and broadcast. However, future newsrooms will have additional and different layers. Some news sites will continue to be operated by a few people dedicated only to one format, such as blogging.

News is a perishable commodity. The newspaper staff have to be on their toes to ensure that important news items are processed quickly, to meet the deadlines of publication. Speed is a prerequisite of the newsroom, and its importance in the production of a daily newspaper could not be emphasized enough. Speed is essential in the following aspects of the newspaper production.

- in communication information;
- in processing information;
- in page-designing and layout;
- in printing and production; and
- in packing and distribution.

Rapid transmission of news becomes meaningless, if information being imparted is inaccurate. This might even affect the paper's credibility. In this context the accuracy of the data and apparently minor details of spellings and language, assume importance. Such correction work is done with the help of the computer and 'fax' machines.

The computers are an ideal system for storing data in their memory and this data could be retrieved at a later stage. The computers act as the data banks, and are very useful sources of reference of the newspaper.

The computers permit data maneuverability to suit the needs of the page designer. This might become necessary in the presentation of the same news item in a different format. The computers could even be programmed for an unlimited supply of type faces. Software for a variety of page designs exist and continue to be invented. The typography, thus, is another requirement of the newsrooms.

Q20. What is Computer? Describe the difference between Hardware and Software components of computer system.

Ans. A computer is a device that accepts information (in the form of digitalized data) and manipulates it for some result based on a program or sequence of instructions on how the data is to be processed.

It is an electronic device that manipulates information, or data. It has the ability to store, retrieve and process data. We can use a computer to type documents, send email and browse the Web. We can also use it to handle spreadsheets, accounting, database management, presentations, games and more.

A computer is an automatic electronic apparatus for making calculations, besides storing and processing information. For this, data along with instructions on how to process the same have fed into the computer. That is called the input. The result obtained from the computer after processing of the data is called the output.

The Basic difference between Hardware and Software: There are two ways of looking at it. First is this that Hardware is something which we can see with our eyes and touch whereas Software is something which we don't see and works in the background and definitely we can't touch it. A very practical example of this can be given in the form of VCR. In this case the VCR where the video cassette is put is the hardware whereas the video cassette which has the film in it can be called as Software. Without each other, they have no value. We cannot run video cassette without a VCR and VCR is nothing but a machine in itself has no movie to run.

Similarly in computers Hardware and Software go neck-in-neck. They are totally dependent upon each other. This is why when we buy a software, it has the hardware requirements mentioned on it since without that much of hardware, it will not work. But, software is a very vast field. Lots and lots of software are available, which one would suit our requirement, we have to use it according to our needs.

Hardware Components of a Computer System

- **Input device** are those parts of a computer, which are used to feed information and instructions to it. There are the keyboard, key punch, card reader, etc.

  The function of the standard typewriter-style keyboard is to convert information to the electronic signals that represent different letters of the alphabet, characters and numbers.

- **Central Processing Unit** (CPU) is the main part of the computer. Processing of information and calculation of data take place here. It is made up of the following three sub-units:

  – Memory,

  – The Control Unit, and

  – The Arithmetic and Logic Unit.

The memory is a device that could receive and store data. Later, this data could be produced on demand, i.e., retrieved.

The control unit of the CPU coordinates the execution the programmed instructions by first selecting the order in which they are to be performed, and then directing them to the other components to execute the necessary action.

The A.L.U. is a sub-unit of CPU, which performs arithmetical calculations, and makes logical decisions.

- **The output devices** are those parts of a computer through which one could get the final output, and which enable us to observe the actual processing of information. These are the screen or the Visual Display Unit (VDU) and the printer. The VDU is a monitor which is used to display the input data and the CPU the output of the processed information.

Software Components of a Computer System: If a computer is to process any information, it must receive instructions of what information to process, where to get that information from, how to process it, and where to display or present the result.

Instructions written for use by a computer are called a program or computer software. Without such a program, a computer cannot do anything.

The term 'software' includes all the computer programs encoded in the computer language. These programs are commercially sold as packages, and obtain very precise instructions to carry out specific tasks. The trained software consultants prepare such programs according to the requirements of their clientale.

The terms 'information' or 'data' include all the facts and figures that record an event, situation or activity. The 'processing' is any activity done by a computer that might involve calculations, classifications, sorting out or manipulation operations on information and data.

The basic steps involved in a certain program are mentioned here, as:

- **Algorithm:** After identifying a task, a finite sequence of procedures is formulated. It is made up of mathematical and/or logical operations designed to solve the problem or task. This sequence is called an Algorithm and it is written in English.
- **Flowchart:** The next step is to prepare a flowchart. It is a diagramatic representation of the steps previously written

down in an algorithm to solve a problem. A standard set of symbols are used to represent various operations. The order, in which these operations are to be executed, is indicated when writing the computer programs. The flowchart is then translated into a program written in computer language. A package like 'NEWS' is capable of providing various fonts and typefaces that could be used in a newspaper office.

A variety of software packages are available in the market place. The software consultants might have to be approached to help select the most appropriate choice.

Q21. Briefly describe 'The Word Processing System'.

Ans. Word processing is the use of computers to create, edit, proofread, format, and print documents. It is a term used to give emphasis on the manipulation of certain types of data characters to form words, sentences and reports. Word processing transforms ideas or useful information into a communication format acceptable to the user and is carried out through the combined efforts of people, hardware and specialized software.

The word-processing is a tool, which assists the user while compiling reports, especially in a newspaper office where enormous amounts of written material keep arriving at the desk. The text is first fed into the computer, and the word-processing software is then used to rearrange it in a required format. This could mean any combination of the following functions:

- To set the left and right margins of a column;
- To set the top and bottom margins of a column;
- To prepare the headlines and footnotes;
- To realign and even auto align words, sentences for paragraphs;
- To underline certain words;
- To print certain words in bold characters;
- To correct or even delete portions of the text;
- To provide a variety of typefaces; and
- To rearrange spacing between lines.

The word-processing software packages are indispensable on another count. These help in preparing pages for publication at a faster rate.

Q22. What is desktop publishing? Discuss the advantages and limitation of using DTP.

Ans. The term desktop publishing describes the process of producing a document using a personal computer. DTP software, once called page assembly software, makes it possible to combine both print and graphics on a single page. Once a user creates a desktop publishing document, he or she can then print a copy using a computer printer, a photocopy machine, or a professional press. DTP also provides the option of creating a digital publication. This allows readers to view a document using a computer monitor rather than a paper copy. DTP requires a wide variety of skills, including an understanding of typography, graphics, layout, and business expectations.

Desktop publishing has been called the grandchild of the typewriter and the child of the electronic typewriter—controlled by a computer. It is a very user-friendly device—essentially a system used for composing pages. In short, it is a means of producing screen based 'WYSIWYG' (What you see is what you get), camera-ready copy and/or camera-ready art work without recourse to cut and paste. Desktop Publishing allows us to run a publishing company from our desk. It enables one person to do everything that normally goes on in a publisher's office, from writing the material, choosing the type, in which the words will be set, designing the pages and then producing the finished pages on a printer.

Benefits of DTP: The DTP has many advantages in comparison with the manual process. It is a factual and can quickly edit with minimum mistakes. Text and graphics can be merged into single file. Achieve higher productivity, efficiency and quality in printing and publishing with economy. DTP is used for type- setting, layout, printing, graphics and photographs etc. With the latest DTP software packages it is possible to undertake a variety of work in the field of printing and publishing. There are some other advantages these are as follows:

- **Simplification of the Process of Publishing:** The entire process of publishing can now be consummated at the desktop without a need to move papers and other materials from desk to desk. The process has been so simplified that with proper training, few people can accomplish with greater efficiency and effectiveness tasks usually handled by many people.

- **Interactiveness:** DTP is such an interactive process that a user finds help readily available as the need arises. A user is prompted by the computer and the response to such promptings guides the computer in providing further assistance to the user. Tasks which a user cannot understand are explained by the computer, thereby providing further education, enlightenment and mentoring. It is rare for a user to get to a cross-road without any form of support to get out from the computer system.
- **Speed:** The speed of the computer is amazing. The computer easily performs tasks that could take human beings a long time to accomplish in a few seconds. This fast forwards production time, making it possible for jobs to be delivered on time. The time gained can be converted into other profitable uses.
- **Storage and Retrieval:** With DTP, a large volume of materials can be stored in the system and retrieved for future use as the need arises. For example, instead of manually storing story files, pictures, etc, they can be safely and conveniently accommodated on the computer system and retrieved for use at the appropriate time.
- **Neatness and Beauty of Final Print:** The final output of the printed work is supposed to be neater and more beautiful, all things being equal. The accuracy and precision of the computer are supposed to eliminate redundancy and other elements that can affect neatness .The variety of types, fonts ,etc, that are available on the computer also gives those utilizing DTP an opportunity to create or enhance beauty through an intelligent combination of various visual elements for aesthetic enhancement.
- **Cost-Effectiveness:** Using DTP can save lot of costs. For example, by reducing the number of people working to get a task accomplished, or by reducing the number of man-hours required for a given task, the publisher is able to save cost on personnel. This saving can then be invested in staff welfare and other things to enhance profit. Human errors are also drastically reduced by the ability of the computer to provide

prompts as the need arises. So, although it may initially appear expensive to use DTP, on the long run, it is more cost-effective.

- **On-line Dissemination:** It is easier and more convenient to upload the published matter on to the Internet for wider dissemination if DTP is used in publishing it. If a matter is published using a process that does not involve computer typesetting, the material would still need to be computer-typeset before being put on the worldwide web. But since DTP is computer-based, the materials are steps ahead in terms of their readiness to be uploaded to the net.

Limitations: Few limitations persist in the new DTP packages too. These are listed below:

- It is not possible to obtain on the VDU an exact copy of the colours, as they would appear in the final print.
- The monitor is capable of showing the character in white against a background, whereas the actual product is black or white.
- The monitor shows only restricted areas of each page. Such fragmented views make it difficult for an entire page to be visualized.
- A change once made in the typography might not eventually be printed as the package would not be programmed for it.

Feedback is the breakfast of Champions.

Ken Blanchard

You can Help other students.
"Inform any error or mistake in this book."

We and Universe
will reward you for Your Kind act.

Email at : feedback@gullybaba.com
or
WhatsApp on 9350849407

Question Papers

Reporting, Writing and Editing: JMC-03

December, 2018

Note: Attempt any five questions. All questions carry equal marks.

Q1. Why should a reporter treat sources as 'sacred'? Do you think the importance of sources has been compromised in today's times? Justify your answer with suitable examples.

Q2. What is the importance of an Interview? How would you prepare to interview a sportsperson/leader?

Q3. What are the precautions a reporter must take while covering court stories?

Q4. What is the style in sports writing? Also explain the need of specialisation for a sports reporter.

Q5. Write a feature (not more than a 1000 words) on the need for Internet connectivity in India.

Q6. What is an editorial? How has the edit page been affected by competition and media market in the current times?

Q7. What is the difference in presentation of news on radio and in print media? Explain with examples.

Q8. What is development reporting? What are the specialised skills required for development reporting? Give suitable examples.

Q9. Explain the qualities and duties of a copy editor.

Q10. How have-market readership changes led to a change in content and design of newspapers today? Explain.

❑❑❑

Reporting, Writing and Editing: JMC-03

June, 2019

Note: Attempt any five questions. All questions carry equal marks.

Q1. Discuss the various sources of News. What care will you take to ensure the reliability and accuracy of the source?

Q2. What type of skills will be required for interviewing a celebrity of your choice?

Q3. What precautions will you take while reporting court proceedings? Discuss with examples.

Q4. Define Development reporting. Discuss the skills required for covering development reporting in the Indian context.

Q5. Write short notes on the following:

(a) Inverted pyramid

(b) Science feature

(c) Story idea

(d) Lead

(e) Attribution

Q6. Discuss the characteristics of Editorials. What is the difference between editorial and other newspaper writing?

Q7. What is the process of compilation of news for radio news bulletin?

Q8. What kind of preparation will you make for interviewing a public figure for a television? Discuss in detail.

Q9. Discuss the role and responsibilities of a copy editor in a newspaper organization.

Q10. Write short notes on the following:

(a) Letter to editor

(b) Headline

(c) News values

(d) Circulation

(e) Captions

❑❑❑

Reporting, Writing and Editing: JMC-03
December, 2019

Note: Attempt any five questions. All questions carry equal marks.

Q1. 'Newspapers have become views papers'. Do you agree with the statement? Substantiate your answer.

Q2. Explain the interviewing skills required for interviewing a sports person.

Q3. Describe the sources required for science and technology reporting. Cite suitable examples in Indian context.

Q4. Define development reporting. How is reporting development stories for the press different from reporting for television?

Q5. Write short notes on:

(a) Humorous lead

(b) Human interest feature

(c) Pool Copy

(d) Photo editing

(e) Off the record

Q6. What is freelance journalism? Explain the ethical considerations in freelance writing.

Q7. Discuss the presentation techniques required for radio news with suitable examples.

Q8. How is writing for television different from writing for newspapers? Discuss.

Q9. What is page designing? Explain the software used for page make-up.

Q10. Write short notes on any two of the following:

(a) Objective reporting

(b) Desk management

(c) Graphics and illustrations

(d) Recce

(e) Travelogue

❑❑❑

Reporting, Writing and Editing: JMC-03

June, 2020

Note: Attempt any five questions. All questions carry equal marks.

Q1. What are the ingredients of news? What changes have come in news making in the current times?

Q2. What precautions would you take while reporting communal conflicts? Cite suitable examples from Indian context.

Q3. What precautions would you exercise while covering court stories? Explain with relevant examples.

Q4. How can science and technology reporting affect social attitudes? Explain with reference to health communication.

Q5. Write a 400 - 500 words feature on one of the following:

(i) Rising Pollution Levels

(ii) Swachch Bharat Abhiyaan

Q6. Explain the difference between various forms of newspaper writing on the following, editorials columns features and letters to editor highlighting the importance of each.

Q7. Why is radio called the medium for the ear? How is news for radio different from news for a newspaper? Explain the differences with examples.

Q8. What kind of research is required before conducting a 1V interview of a famous literature personality? Write down ten questions you would ask a literature personality of your choice.

Q9. What are the duties and qualities of a copy editor?

Q10. How does design help in sales promotion of a periodical? List down some strategies for a local magazine in your area to increase the profit.

Reporting, Writing and Editing: JMC-03

December, 2020

Note: (i) Attempt any five questions. (ii) All questions carry equal marks.

Q1. What is Investigative Reporting? How is it different from interpretative reporting? What is ethical debate around investigative reporting?

Q2. Design a set of 15 questions you would like to ask the Finance Minister of India about budget.

Q3. Write short notes on the following (word limit 150 words each):

(a) Papers laid on the table of the house

(b) Zero hour

(c) No confidence motion

(d) Starred and unstarred questions

Q4. What are the news values followed in any sports news story? List down the points to be included in the coverage of your favourite sport.

Q5. Write any one of the following in 500 words on a topic of your choice:

(a) A human interest feature

(b) A travel sketch

Q6. Write short notes on the following (word limit 150 words each):

(i) Freelancing **(ii) Stringer**

(iii) News analysis **(iv) Magazine Writing**

Q7. Write the script of a radio feature on a topic of your choice, in 400-500 words.

Q8. Differentiate between TV Script and Radio Script. Explain with respect to concept, treatment and editing.

Q9. Write short notes on the following (word limit 150 words each):

(i) Graphic illustrations **(ii) Cropping**

(iii) Caption writing **(iv) Photo editing**

Q10. How has technology impacted the newspaper industry? Explain with suitable examples.

❑❑❑

Reporting, Writing and Editing: JMC-03

June, 2021

Note: Attempt any five questions. All questions carry equal marks.

Q1. "Every development has the potential to become news." Justify the statement in the light of any five ingredients of news. Explain with suitable examples.

Q2. "Complete objectivity in news is a myth." Do you agree? Justify the statement in the light of current trends of news reporting.

Q3. What is Contempt of Court? What precautions must a legal reporter take while covering court stories?

Q4. Why is science communication important for the society? What can be the possible sources for a science reporter and what kind of language should be used in science stories for popular appeal?

Q5. Explain the techniques of good writing with examples.

Q6. What is an Editorial? Explain its characteristics and types.

Q7. What are the roles of Bulletin editors and Radio reporters? Explain in detail.

Q8. How is news in television different from that in radio and newspapers? Discuss the techniques of TV news reporting.

Q9. How should one edit a copy? Explain the duties of a copy editor.

Q10. What are various features of the front page design of a daily newspaper? Explain in context of a daily newspaper of your choice.

❑❑❑

Reporting, Writing and Editing: JMC-03

December, 2021

Note: Attempt any five questions. All questions carry equal marks.

Q1. What is 'Nose for News'? Why is the ability to cope with pressure from outside and within the news organisation an important quality for reporters? Explain in context of profit-oriented modern media.

Q2. "An interview is a conversation with a strategy." Justify the statement with the help of suitable examples.

Q3. What breaches of privilege should a legal reporter take care of? Explain with examples.

Q4. Define sustainable development. Explain the process of development and the styles of development reporting.

Q5. Write a human interest feature in 400 words on a topic of your choice.

Q6. What is the difference between an article and a review? Write the review of a book you have recently read, in 300 words.

Q7. What is the importance of language, content, voice and rhythm in a radio programme? Explain with examples.

Q8. Write the beginning and ending script of a TV documentary on Jammu and Kashmir.

Q9. What are the qualities of a good photographer? Why are graphic illustrations important for a newspaper?

Q10. What is the difference in page layout and design of a daily newspaper as compared to a magazine? Explain their strategies for self-promotion.

❑❑❑

Reporting, Writing and Editing: JMC-03

June, 2022

Note: (i) Attempt any five questions. (ii) All questions carry equal marks.

Q1. What are news values? Explain the fundamental characteristics of news with examples.

Q2. What are the essential qualities of a reporter that make him/her competent for the profession?

Q3. What is Contempt of Court? Explain the journalistic defences against it.

Q4. Explain the meaning and concept of development reporting. What are the specialised skills required for development reporting?

Q5. Explain any five types of leads with examples.

Q6. What is the difference between an article, feature and analysis? How can one generate ideas for magazine writing?

Q7. How is the language of speech different from that of writing? Explain the ingredients of a good radio script.

Q8. What is Photo Editing? What is the difference between captions and graphic illustrations? Explain the qualities of a good photographer.

❑❑❑

www.ingramcontent.com/pod-product-compliance
Ingram Content Group UK Ltd.
Pitfield, Milton Keynes, MK11 3LW, UK
UKHW021703190726
13853UKWH00001B/404

9 789383 921348